Out of the Box Teaching

A Teacher's handbook

Dr. Reni Francis

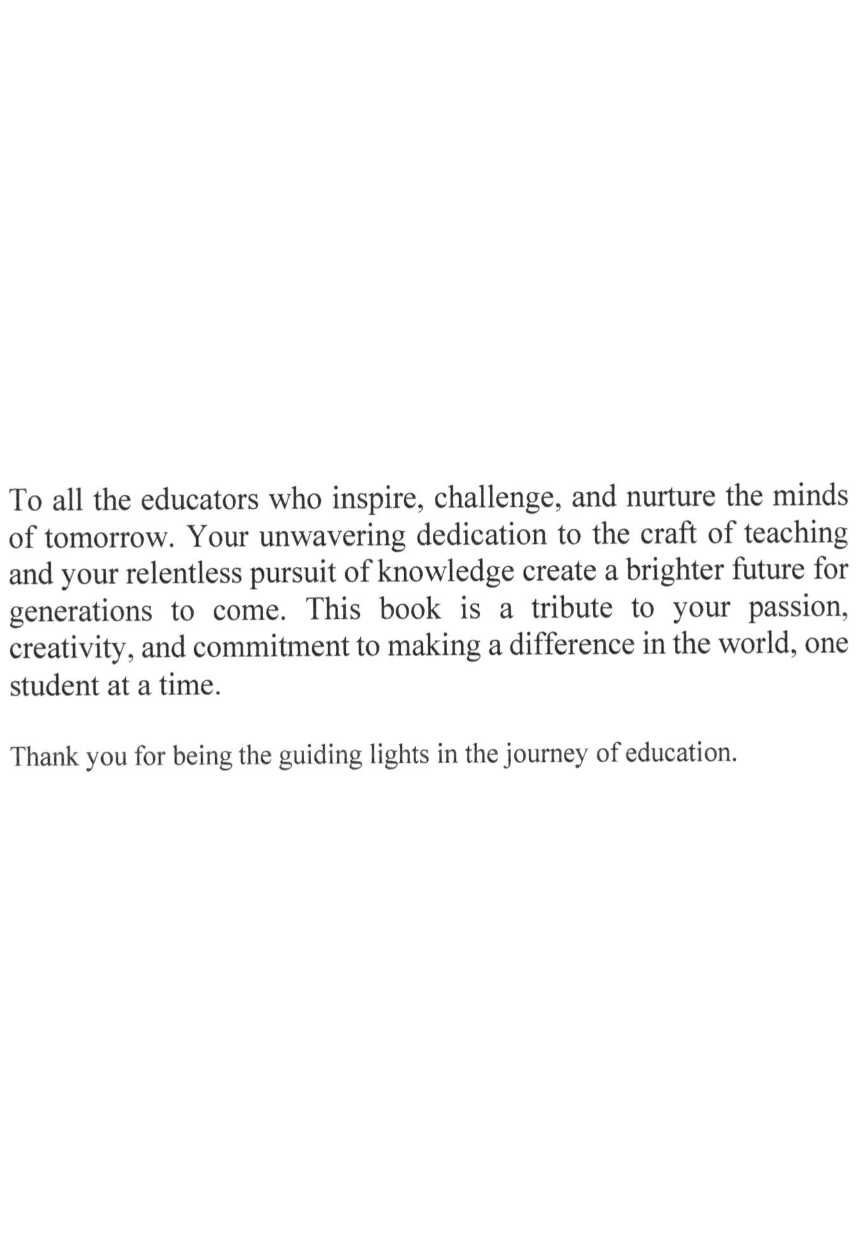

To all the educators who inspire, challenge, and nurture the minds of tomorrow. Your unwavering dedication to the craft of teaching and your relentless pursuit of knowledge create a brighter future for generations to come. This book is a tribute to your passion, creativity, and commitment to making a difference in the world, one student at a time.

Thank you for being the guiding lights in the journey of education.

Contents

1. Lecture Method

2. Lecture cum Discussion

3. Interactive Lecture

4. Just in Time Teaching

5. Experiential Learning

6. Case Study Method

7. Inquiry based Learning

8. Problem based Learning

9. Project based Learning

10. Scenario based Learning

11. Role Play/ Dramatization

12. Simulation

13. Field Work / Onsite Learning

14. Seminar Method

15. Demonstration Method

16. Scaffolding Method

17. Group Work/Participative Method

18. Tutorial Method

19.Correlational / Integrative Method

20.Constructivist Method

21. Socratic Questioning

22. Theme Based Learning

23. Project Method

24. Programmed Instruction

25. Heuristic Method

Preface

Education is the cornerstone of a progressive society, shaping the minds and futures of individuals who will become tomorrow's leaders, innovators, and change-makers. As we navigate through an era characterized by rapid technological advancements and an ever-changing global landscape, the role of educators has never been more vital. This book, "Out of the Box Teaching," is born out of a deep recognition of the need for dynamic, adaptable, and effective teaching strategies.

Over the years, I have had the privilege of working with educators, students, and educational leaders from various backgrounds and settings. This experience has underscored the importance of not only mastering traditional teaching methods but also embracing innovative approaches that cater to the diverse needs of students. Each classroom is a unique ecosystem, and the ability to adapt teaching methods to engage and inspire all learners is essential.

This book explores ten distinct teaching methods, each offering a unique pathway to student engagement and learning. From the traditional lecture method to cutting-edge approaches like Just-in-Time Teaching and Project-Based Learning, this book provides comprehensive insights into the theory and practice of each method. Through detailed explanations, step-by-step guides, and real-life classroom scenarios, readers will gain practical tools and strategies to enhance their teaching practices.

The aim of "Innovative Pedagogy" is not only to inform but also to inspire educators to explore, experiment, and innovate in their teaching. By blending proven techniques with new, creative approaches, we can create dynamic learning environments that foster critical thinking, collaboration, and real-world application of knowledge.

To all the educators reading this book, I hope it serves as a valuable resource in your professional journey. May it empower you to create engaging, inclusive, and transformative learning experiences for your students. Your dedication to education is shaping a brighter future, and for that, I am deeply grateful.

Thank you for joining me on this journey of exploration and innovation in teaching.

Sincerely,

Dr. Reni Francis

Acknowledgments

This book is the culmination of the efforts, insights, and support of many individuals, and I am deeply grateful to everyone who contributed to its creation.

First and foremost, I extend my heartfelt thanks to all the educators who have inspired and influenced my understanding of teaching and learning. Your passion, dedication, and innovative spirit have been a constant source of inspiration. Special thanks to my colleagues and mentors who have shared their wisdom and experiences, enriching my perspective on effective teaching practices.

I am immensely grateful to the students I have had the privilege of teaching and learning from over the years. Your curiosity, creativity, and resilience have continually reminded me of the profound impact of education. This book is, in many ways, a reflection of our shared learning journey.

I would like to express my sincere appreciation to the educational institutions and organizations that have supported my work. Your commitment to fostering excellence in education has provided a fertile ground for the development and dissemination of innovative teaching methods.

ACKNOWLEDGMENTS

To my family and friends, your unwavering support and encouragement have been invaluable. Thank you for believing in me and for providing the love and understanding that sustained me through the writing process.

A special thank you to the editorial team, whose expertise and meticulous attention to detail have greatly enhanced the quality of this book. Your guidance and feedback have been instrumental in bringing this project to fruition.

Finally, I am deeply grateful to all the readers of this book. Your interest in exploring diverse teaching methods is a testament to your dedication to providing the best possible education for your students. I hope this book serves as a valuable resource in your teaching journey.

Thank you all for being a part of this endeavor. Together, we are contributing to a brighter future through education.

With gratitude,

Dr. Reni Francis

Introduction

In the rapidly evolving world of education, one thing remains constant: the profound impact that effective teaching has on student learning and development. The modern classroom is a dynamic environment, characterized by diverse student needs, varying learning styles, and an abundance of information and resources. To navigate this complexity and ensure that all students are engaged and successful, educators must be equipped with a broad repertoire of teaching methods.

"Out of the Box Teaching" is designed to be a comprehensive guide for educators who are committed to enhancing their teaching practices. This book explores ten distinct teaching methods, each offering unique strategies and approaches to foster student engagement, critical thinking, and real-world application of knowledge.

Purpose of the Book

The primary goal of this book is to provide educators with practical tools and insights that can be immediately applied in the classroom. By understanding the theory and practice behind various teaching methods, educators can make informed decisions about which approaches are best suited to their specific teaching contexts and student populations.

Education is the foundation upon which societies are built, and the methods used to impart knowledge have evolved significantly over the centuries. In today's rapidly changing world, the importance of innovative teaching methods cannot be overstated. These methods are crucial for engaging diverse student populations, fostering critical thinking, and preparing learners for the complexities of the modern world.

Historical Evolution of Teaching Methods

Ancient and Medieval Periods

In ancient times, education was often an elite privilege, focusing on oral traditions and memorization. Socratic questioning, a method named after the philosopher Socrates, was an early form of interactive learning, encouraging critical thinking through dialogue.

During the medieval period, the lecture method became prominent in universities. Knowledge was delivered by a single teacher to a passive audience of students. This period saw limited interaction and was primarily centered on religious and classical texts.

Renaissance and Enlightenment

The Renaissance brought a renewed interest in classical learning and humanism. Teaching methods began to incorporate more discussion and debate, reflecting the period's emphasis on critical thinking and exploration.

The Enlightenment further advanced educational practices, promoting reason and scientific inquiry. Figures like Jean-Jacques Rousseau emphasized experiential learning, arguing that education should nurture a child's natural curiosity and development.

19th and Early 20th Centuries

The 19th century introduced more structured and systematic approaches to education. The advent of the industrial revolution necessitated education for the masses, leading to the establishment of public schooling systems. Methods such as the monitorial system, where older students taught younger ones, were used to manage large classrooms efficiently.

The early 20th century saw the influence of educational theorists like John Dewey, who championed progressive education. Dewey advocated for learning by doing, emphasizing the need for education to be relevant to students' lives and experiences.

Late 20th Century to Present

The latter half of the 20th century brought significant advancements in educational psychology and pedagogy. Constructivist theories, influenced by Piaget and Vygotsky, emphasized the importance of active learning and social interaction in knowledge construction.

The digital revolution of the late 20th and early 21st centuries has transformed education dramatically. Technology has introduced new teaching methods such as flipped classrooms, blended learning, and online education, making learning more accessible and interactive.

Importance of Innovative Teaching Methods Today

Engagement and Motivation:

Innovative teaching methods cater to diverse learning styles and preferences, making learning more engaging and motivating for students. Active learning strategies, such as project-based and experiential learning, foster a deeper connection to the material.

Critical Thinking and Problem-Solving:

Methods like inquiry-based learning and problem-based learning encourage students to think critically and solve complex problems. These skills are essential for success in the 21st-century workforce.

Collaboration and Communication:

Collaborative teaching methods, such as group projects and scenario-based learning, help students develop communication and teamwork skills. These abilities are vital in a globalized and interconnected world.

Adaptability and Lifelong Learning:

In a rapidly changing world, the ability to adapt and learn continuously is crucial. Innovative teaching methods prepare students to be lifelong learners, equipping them with the skills to navigate new challenges and opportunities.

Technology Integration:

The integration of technology in education allows for personalized learning experiences and access to a vast array of resources. Methods like Just-in-Time Teaching and interactive lectures leverage technology to enhance learning and address individual student needs.

Conclusion

The evolution of teaching methods over the centuries reflects a growing understanding of how people learn best. From the oral traditions of ancient times to the technologically enhanced classrooms of today, each era has contributed to the development of more effective and inclusive educational practices. In "Innovative Pedagogy: Exploring Diverse Teaching Methods for the Modern Classroom," we delve into these progressive approaches, providing educators with the tools to create dynamic, engaging, and effective learning environments. By embracing innovative teaching methods, we can better prepare students for the challenges and opportunities of the future.

1. Lecture Method

Meaning: The lecture method is a traditional teaching approach where the teacher presents information verbally to a group of students. This method involves a teacher-centered delivery where the primary mode of communication is through spoken words, often accompanied by visual aids like slides or whiteboard illustrations.

Purpose:

1. **Impart Knowledge:** To deliver comprehensive and detailed information on a subject.
2. **Cover Extensive Material:** To efficiently cover a large amount of content in a limited time.
3. **Introduce New Topics:** To provide a foundation and context for further learning.
4. **Clarify Complex Concepts:** To explain difficult concepts in a structured and clear manner.
5. **Set Learning Objectives:** To outline the key points and objectives of the lesson.

Steps with Examples:

1. **Preparation:**
   - Example: A biology teacher prepares a lecture on cell division, organizing key points, creating a PowerPoint presentation, and gathering visual aids like diagrams of mitosis and meiosis.

2. **Introduction:**
   - Example: The teacher begins the class by introducing the topic of cell division, explaining its importance in growth and reproduction, and outlining the objectives of the lesson.

3. **Presentation:**
   - Example: The teacher delivers the lecture, explaining each stage of mitosis and meiosis, using slides to show diagrams and animations of the processes.

4. **Interaction:**
   - Example: Throughout the lecture, the teacher asks students questions to keep them engaged, such as "What happens during metaphase?" or "Can anyone explain the difference between mitosis and meiosis?"

5. **Summary:**
   - Example: At the end of the lecture, the teacher summarizes the key points, reiterating the stages of cell division and their significance.

6. **Q&A Session:**
   - Example: The teacher invites students to ask questions, providing clarification on any confusing points and ensuring understanding.

Criteria:

- **Clarity:** The content should be presented in a clear and understandable manner.
- **Organization:** The lecture should follow a logical sequence, with a clear introduction, body, and conclusion.
- **Engagement:** The teacher should actively engage students through questions and discussions.
- **Visual Aids:** Effective use of visual aids to enhance understanding.

Role of Teacher with Classroom Examples:

- **Presenter:**
  - Example: In a history class, the teacher presents a lecture on the causes of World War II, detailing the political and economic factors involved.
- **Organizer:**
  - Example: The teacher organizes the lecture content chronologically, starting from the Treaty of Versailles to the invasion of Poland.

- **Facilitator:**
  - Example: During the lecture, the teacher facilitates understanding by explaining complex concepts like appeasement and totalitarianism.
- **Evaluator:**
  - Example: The teacher evaluates student comprehension by asking questions and encouraging discussion at the end of the lecture.

Merits and Demerits with Examples:

- **Merits:**
  - **Efficient Coverage:**
    - Example: A chemistry teacher can cover the entire periodic table in a few lectures, providing a comprehensive overview of elements and their properties.
  - **Teacher Control:**
    - Example: The teacher can control the pace of the lesson, ensuring that all key points are covered thoroughly.
  - **Structured Learning:**
    - Example: Students receive information in a well-organized format, which helps in building a solid foundation of knowledge.

- o **Scalability:**
  - Example: A single teacher can deliver a lecture to a large group of students, making it a cost-effective teaching method.
- **Demerits:**
  - o **Passive Learning:**
    - Example: Students may become passive recipients of information, leading to lower retention and engagement.
  - o **Limited Interaction:**
    - Example: In a large lecture hall, individual student participation and interaction are minimal, reducing opportunities for personalized learning.
  - o **One-Size-Fits-All:**
    - Example: The lecture method may not cater to the diverse learning styles of all students, such as those who learn better through hands-on activities or group work.
  - o **Monotony:**
    - Example: Listening to a long lecture without breaks or interactive elements can become monotonous, leading to decreased attention and interest.

Classroom Scenarios:

1. **History Lecture on World War II:**
   - The teacher presents a detailed timeline of events leading up to World War II, using maps and historical documents to illustrate key points.

2. **Biology Lecture on Photosynthesis:**
   - The teacher explains the process of photosynthesis, using diagrams to show the light-dependent and light-independent reactions.

3. **Physics Lecture on Newton's Laws:**
   - The teacher demonstrates Newton's three laws of motion with practical examples and video clips of experiments.

4. **Literature Lecture on Shakespeare:**
   - The teacher analyzes the themes and characters in "Macbeth," reading excerpts from the play and discussing its historical context.

The lecture method, while traditional, can be highly effective when used appropriately. Combining it with interactive elements and visual aids can enhance student engagement and understanding.

2. Lecture cum Discussion

Meaning and Definition: Lecture cum discussion is a hybrid teaching method that combines traditional lecturing with interactive discussion. The teacher delivers content in segments, interspersing the lecture with questions and discussion to encourage student participation and deepen understanding.

Purpose:

- To provide structured content delivery while engaging students in active learning.
- To promote critical thinking and better retention through discussion.

Steps with Examples:

1. **Preparation:**
   - Example: A sociology teacher prepares a lecture on social inequality, organizing key points and discussion questions.

2. **Introduction:**
   - Example: The teacher introduces the topic, explaining the importance of understanding social inequality and the objectives of the lesson.

3. **Presentation and Discussion:**

   - Example: The teacher presents the first segment of the lecture on economic inequality, then pauses to ask students their opinions on the impact of income disparity on society.

4. **Continued Presentation and Discussion:**

   - Example: The teacher continues with the next segment on educational inequality, prompting students to discuss how access to education can influence social mobility.

5. **Summary and Q&A:**

   - Example: The teacher summarizes the key points, reiterates the main discussion highlights, and invites further questions.

Criteria:

- Balance between lecture and discussion.
- Clear and organized content.
- Effective questioning techniques.
- Encouragement of student participation.

Role of Teacher with Classroom Examples:

- **Facilitator:**
  - Example: The teacher facilitates discussion by asking open-ended questions, such as "How do you think economic inequality affects social cohesion?"
- **Presenter:**
  - Example: The teacher delivers content clearly, ensuring students understand the material before moving on to discussion.
- **Moderator:**
  - Example: The teacher moderates the discussion, ensuring it stays on topic and all students have the opportunity to contribute.
- **Evaluator:**
  - Example: The teacher evaluates student contributions during the discussion to gauge their understanding.

Merits and Demerits with Examples:

- **Merits:**
  - **Enhanced Understanding:**
    - Example: Discussing real-world implications of social inequality helps students understand theoretical concepts better.

- o **Student Engagement:**
  - ▪ Example: Regular discussion breaks keep students engaged and attentive.
- o **Critical Thinking:**
  - ▪ Example: Analyzing and debating different viewpoints fosters critical thinking skills.
- o **Immediate Feedback:**
  - ▪ Example: Students receive immediate feedback on their understanding during discussions.

- • **Demerits:**
  - o **Time-Consuming:**
    - ▪ Example: Balancing lecture and discussion may require more time, potentially limiting content coverage.
  - o **Classroom Management:**
    - ▪ Example: Managing discussions in large classes can be challenging.
  - o **Off-Topic Discussions:**
    - ▪ Example: Discussions may sometimes veer off-topic, requiring the teacher to steer them back.

- o **Variable Participation:**
  - ▪ Example: Some students may dominate discussions while others remain passive.

Classroom Scenarios:

1. **Economics Class on Supply and Demand:**
   - o The teacher explains the basics of supply and demand, then pauses to discuss real-world examples like gas prices.

2. **Psychology Class on Cognitive Development:**
   - o The teacher presents Piaget's stages of cognitive development and then discusses with students their observations of children's behavior.

3. **Environmental Science Class on Climate Change:**
   - o The teacher explains the greenhouse effect and then engages students in a discussion on potential solutions to climate change.

4. **Literature Class on Symbolism in "The Great Gatsby":**
   - o The teacher analyzes symbols in the novel and then discusses with students their interpretations of these symbols.

5. **History Class on the Cold War:**
   - o The teacher presents key events of the Cold War and then discusses with students the impact of these events on modern geopolitics.

3. Interactive Lecture

Meaning: An interactive lecture incorporates elements of student participation within the lecture, such as questions, activities, and technology-based interactions.

Purpose:

- To make lectures more engaging and interactive.
- To improve retention and understanding of material.

Steps with Examples:

1. **Preparation:**
   - Example: A physics teacher prepares an interactive lecture on Newton's laws of motion, including demonstrations and interactive simulations.

2. **Introduction:**
   - Example: The teacher introduces the topic and explains the interactive elements to be used during the lecture.

3. **Interactive Content Delivery:**
   - Example: The teacher explains Newton's first law, then uses an online simulation to demonstrate inertia, allowing students to manipulate variables.

4. **Student Participation:**
   - Example: The teacher asks students to predict outcomes of different scenarios in the simulation and discuss their observations.

5. **Summary and Reflection:**
   - Example: The teacher summarizes the key points and reflects on the interactive elements, discussing what was learned.

Criteria:

- Regular interactive elements.
- Use of technology to enhance participation.
- Clear instructions for activities.
- Integration of student feedback into the lecture.

Role of Teacher with Classroom Examples:

- **Facilitator:**
  - Example: The teacher facilitates interactive activities, guiding students through simulations and discussions.
- **Presenter:**
  - Example: The teacher presents content clearly and concisely, ensuring students understand the material before interactive elements.

- **Tech-Savvy Guide:**
  - Example: The teacher uses technology effectively, such as simulations and clicker questions, to engage students.
- **Feedback Integrator:**
  - Example: The teacher incorporates student feedback from interactive elements into the lecture to clarify concepts.

Merits and Demerits with Examples:

- **Merits:**
  - **Increased Engagement:**
    - Example: Interactive simulations of physics experiments keep students engaged and interested.
  - **Better Retention:**
    - Example: Participating in interactive activities helps students remember concepts better.
  - **Catering to Different Learning Styles:**
    - Example: Interactive elements like simulations and discussions cater to visual and auditory learners.

- o **Immediate Feedback:**
    - ▪ Example: Students receive immediate feedback on their understanding through interactive quizzes and polls.
- **Demerits:**
  - o **Preparation Time:**
    - ▪ Example: Preparing interactive elements and simulations requires additional time and effort.
  - o **Technology Dependence:**
    - ▪ Example: Technical issues with simulations or clicker systems can disrupt the lecture.
  - o **Classroom Management:**
    - ▪ Example: Managing interactive activities in large classes can be challenging.
  - o **Varied Student Participation:**
    - ▪ Example: Some students may be more enthusiastic about interactive elements than others.

Classroom Scenarios:

1. **Chemistry Lecture on Chemical Reactions:**
   - The teacher uses an online lab simulation to demonstrate different types of chemical reactions, allowing students to experiment virtually.

2. **History Lecture on Ancient Civilizations:**
   - The teacher incorporates interactive maps and timelines, asking students to explore different aspects of ancient cultures.

3. **Biology Lecture on Human Anatomy:**
   - The teacher uses a 3D anatomy app to show different body systems, allowing students to explore the structures interactively.

4. **Mathematics Lecture on Calculus:**
   - The teacher uses an interactive graphing tool to demonstrate concepts of differentiation and integration, involving students in manipulating graphs.

5. **Economics Lecture on Market Structures:**
   - The teacher uses clicker questions to poll students on different market scenarios, discussing the implications of their responses.

4. Just in Time Teaching

Meaning and Definition: Just in Time Teaching (JiTT) is an instructional strategy that blends web-based learning with classroom activities. It involves collecting student feedback on pre-class assignments and adjusting teaching based on their responses just before class.

Purpose:

- To tailor classroom activities based on student understanding and needs.
- To increase engagement and learning efficiency.

Steps with Examples:

1. **Pre-Class Assignments:**
   - Example: A chemistry teacher assigns pre-class reading on chemical bonding and asks students to complete an online quiz.

2. **Collect and Analyze Responses:**
   - Example: The teacher reviews the quiz responses to identify common misconceptions and areas where students struggled.

3. **Adjust Lesson Plan:**

   o Example: Based on the quiz analysis, the teacher adjusts the lesson plan to focus more on ionic and covalent bonding, which students found challenging.

4. **Classroom Instruction:**

   o Example: In class, the teacher addresses the misconceptions identified in the quiz and provides additional explanations and examples.

5. **Post-Class Reflection:**

   o Example: After the class, the teacher reflects on the effectiveness of the lesson adjustments and plans future lessons accordingly.

Criteria:

- Effective pre-class assignments.
- Timely analysis of student feedback.
- Flexible lesson planning.
- Integration of feedback into teaching.

Role of Teacher with Classroom Examples:

- **Planner and Coordinator:**

  o Example: The teacher plans pre-class assignments and coordinates the collection and analysis of student responses.

- **Analyzer:**
  - Example: The teacher analyzes quiz responses to identify areas of difficulty and adjusts the lesson plan accordingly.
- **Adaptive Instructor:**
  - Example: The teacher adapts classroom instruction based on student needs and feedback.
- **Reflective Practitioner:**
  - Example: The teacher reflects on the effectiveness of the lesson and plans future instruction based on student feedback.

Merits and Demerits with Examples:

- **Merits:**
  - **Tailored Instruction:**
    - Example: Addressing student misconceptions about chemical bonding directly in class improves understanding.
  - **Increased Engagement:**
    - Example: Students are more engaged when the lesson addresses their specific difficulties.

- o **Active Learning:**
    - Example: Pre-class assignments and in-class adjustments promote active learning.
- o **Immediate Feedback:**
    - Example: Teachers can provide immediate feedback on pre-class quizzes and address issues in real-time.

- **Demerits:**
    - o **Time-Consuming:**
        - Example: Analyzing pre-class responses and adjusting lesson plans can be time-consuming.
    - o **Dependence on Student Participation:**
        - Example: The effectiveness of JiTT depends on students completing pre-class assignments.
    - o **Potential for Overwhelm:**
        - Example: Teachers may feel overwhelmed by the need to continuously adapt lesson plans.
    - o **Technical Issues:**
        - Example: Technical issues with online quizzes or assignments can disrupt the process.

Classroom Scenarios:

1. **Physics Class on Electromagnetism:**
   - The teacher assigns pre-class reading and a quiz on electromagnetic waves, then adjusts the lesson to focus on wave properties that students found difficult.

2. **History Class on the Renaissance:**
   - The teacher assigns a pre-class essay on key Renaissance figures, then uses the responses to guide a class discussion on their contributions.

3. **Biology Class on Genetics:**
   - The teacher assigns pre-class problems on Mendelian genetics, then focuses the lesson on the concepts students struggled with the most.

4. **Mathematics Class on Probability:**
   - The teacher assigns pre-class exercises on probability theory and adjusts the lesson to address common errors and misconceptions.

5. **Economics Class on Supply and Demand:**
   - The teacher assigns pre-class reading and questions on supply and demand, then tailors the lesson to address student difficulties and expand on key concepts.

5. Experiential Learning

Meaning: Experiential learning is a student-centered approach that involves learning through experience and reflection. Students engage in hands-on activities and then reflect on their experiences to gain a deeper understanding of the concepts.

Purpose:

- To promote active learning through real-life experiences.
- To develop critical thinking, problem-solving, and reflective skills.

Steps with Examples:

1. **Planning:**
   - Example: A biology teacher plans a field trip to a local ecosystem to study biodiversity.

2. **Experience:**
   - Example: During the field trip, students collect samples, observe species, and take notes on their findings.

3. **Reflection:**
   - Example: After the field trip, students reflect on their experiences, discussing what they learned and how it relates to classroom concepts.

4. **Conceptualization:**

    o Example: Students connect their field trip observations to theoretical concepts, such as ecosystems and food webs.

5. **Application:**

    o Example: Students design a project or presentation based on their field trip findings, applying their knowledge to a real-world context.

Criteria:

- Hands-on activities.
- Opportunities for reflection and discussion.
- Clear connections to theoretical concepts.
- Application of learning to real-world situations.

Role of Teacher with Classroom Examples:

- **Facilitator:**

    o Example: The teacher facilitates the field trip, guiding students in their observations and data collection.

- **Reflective Coach:**

    o Example: The teacher leads reflection sessions, encouraging students to discuss their experiences and insights.

- **Connector:**
  - Example: The teacher helps students connect their hands-on experiences to classroom concepts.
- **Evaluator:**
  - Example: The teacher assesses student projects and presentations based on their application of knowledge.

Merits and Demerits with Examples:

- **Merits:**
  - **Active Learning:**
    - Example: Students actively engage in learning through field trips and hands-on activities.
  - **Real-World Application:**
    - Example: Connecting classroom concepts to real-world situations enhances understanding and retention.
  - **Skill Development:**
    - Example: Students develop critical thinking, problem-solving, and reflective skills.

- o **Increased Engagement:**
    - Example: Hands-on activities and real-life experiences keep students motivated and interested.
- **Demerits:**
  - o **Resource-Intensive:**
    - Example: Organizing field trips and hands-on activities can be time-consuming and costly.
  - o **Variable Outcomes:**
    - Example: Learning outcomes may vary based on individual student experiences and reflections.
  - o **Logistical Challenges:**
    - Example: Coordinating field trips and ensuring student safety can be challenging.
  - o **Assessment Difficulties:**
    - Example: Assessing experiential learning outcomes can be subjective and complex.

Classroom Scenarios:

1. **Environmental Science Class:**
   - o The teacher organizes a field trip to a nature reserve where students study ecosystems and biodiversity.

2. **History Class:**

   o The teacher arranges a visit to a historical site, such as a museum or battlefield, for students to learn about historical events.

3. **Business Studies Class:**

   o The teacher arranges a visit to a local business, allowing students to observe business operations and interview employees.

4. **Art Class:**

   o The teacher organizes a visit to an art gallery, where students analyze and critique different artworks.

5. **Physics Class:**

   o The teacher sets up a lab experiment where students build and test simple machines, applying concepts of mechanics.

6. Case Study Method

Meaning: The case study method involves students analyzing real-life scenarios or cases to apply theoretical knowledge and develop problem-solving skills. It is a student-centered approach that encourages critical thinking and practical application of concepts.

Purpose:

- To apply theoretical knowledge to real-world situations.
- To develop analytical, decision-making, and problem-solving skills.

Steps with Examples:

1. **Case Selection:**
   - Example: A business teacher selects a case study on a company's marketing strategy for students to analyze.
2. **Background Information:**
   - Example: Students read and understand the background information on the company's marketing strategy, including its objectives, target audience, and challenges.

3. **Analysis:**

   o Example: Students analyze the case, identifying key issues and evaluating different solutions or strategies.

4. **Discussion:**

   o Example: The teacher facilitates a class discussion where students share their analyses and proposed solutions.

5. **Conclusion:**

   o Example: Students summarize their findings and present their conclusions, discussing the implications and lessons learned.

Criteria:

- Realistic and relevant case studies.
- Clear learning objectives.
- Opportunities for analysis and discussion.
- Reflective practices.

Role of Teacher with Classroom Examples:

- **Case Selector:**

   o Example: The teacher selects appropriate and relevant case studies that align with learning objectives.

- **Facilitator:**
  - o Example: The teacher facilitates case discussions, guiding students in their analyses and encouraging diverse perspectives.
- **Evaluator:**
  - o Example: The teacher assesses student analyses and conclusions based on their application of theoretical knowledge.
- **Reflective Coach:**
  - o Example: The teacher encourages students to reflect on their learning experiences and the real-world implications of the case.

Merits and Demerits with Examples:

- **Merits:**
  - o **Real-World Application:**
    - ▪ Example: Analyzing a company's marketing strategy helps students understand the practical application of marketing concepts.
  - o **Skill Development:**
    - ▪ Example: Students develop critical thinking, problem-solving, and decision-making skills through case analysis.

- o **Engagement:**
  - Example: Realistic case studies engage students and make learning more relevant and interesting.
- o **Diverse Perspectives:**
  - Example: Discussing different analyses and solutions fosters collaboration and diverse perspectives.
- **Demerits:**
  - o **Time-Consuming:**
    - Example: Analyzing and discussing case studies can be time-consuming, potentially limiting content coverage.
  - o **Varied Quality:**
    - Example: The quality of case studies can vary, affecting the learning experience.
  - o **Subjectivity:**
    - Example: Assessing case study analyses can be subjective and dependent on individual interpretations.
  - o **Resource-Intensive:**
    - Example: Developing or sourcing high-quality case studies requires time and resources.

Classroom Scenarios:

1. **Business Class on Marketing Strategies:**
   - o The teacher assigns a case study on a company's failed marketing campaign, asking students to analyze what went wrong and propose alternative strategies.

2. **Law Class on Legal Ethics:**
   - o The teacher presents a case study on a controversial legal case, prompting students to discuss the ethical dilemmas involved.

3. **Healthcare Class on Patient Care:**
   - o The teacher assigns a case study on a complex patient care scenario, encouraging students to develop care plans and discuss the implications.

4. **Education Class on Classroom Management:**
   - o The teacher presents a case study on a challenging classroom situation, asking students to propose management strategies and discuss their effectiveness.

5. **Engineering Class on Project Management:**
   - o The teacher assigns a case study on a failed engineering project, prompting students to analyze the project management issues and suggest improvements

7. Inquiry based Learning

Meaning: Inquiry-based learning is a student-centered approach that involves exploring questions, problems, or scenarios. Students develop their understanding by investigating and finding answers through research, experimentation, and critical thinking.

Purpose:

- To foster curiosity and encourage students to take ownership of their learning.
- To develop critical thinking, research, and problem-solving skills.

Steps with Examples:

1. **Question Formulation:**
   - Example: In a science class, students formulate questions about the effects of pollution on local waterways.

2. **Investigation:**
   - Example: Students conduct experiments, collect data, and research scientific literature to answer their questions.

3. **Analysis:**

   o Example: Students analyze their data and findings, identifying patterns and drawing conclusions.

4. **Presentation:**

   o Example: Students present their findings to the class, discussing their methods, results, and implications.

5. **Reflection:**

   o Example: Students reflect on their learning process, discussing what they learned and how they can apply it in the future.

Criteria:

- Student-driven questions.
- Opportunities for research and experimentation.
- Critical analysis and reflection.
- Clear connections to curriculum objectives.

Role of Teacher with Classroom Examples:

- **Facilitator:**

   o Example: The teacher facilitates the inquiry process, guiding students in formulating questions and conducting investigations.

- **Resource Provider:**
  - Example: The teacher provides resources, such as scientific articles and lab equipment, to support student investigations.
- **Mentor:**
  - Example: The teacher mentors students throughout their investigations, providing feedback and support.
- **Evaluator:**
  - Example: The teacher assesses student investigations and presentations based on their research methods, findings, and reflections.

Merits and Demerits with Examples:

- **Merits:**
  - **Student Engagement:**
    - Example: Students are more engaged when they explore questions and topics that interest them.
  - **Skill Development:**
    - Example: Inquiry-based learning develops critical thinking, research, and problem-solving skills.
  - **Ownership of Learning:**
    - Example: Students take ownership of their learning, fostering independence and responsibility.

- o **Deeper Understanding:**
  - Example: Investigating and finding answers to questions leads to a deeper understanding of concepts.

- **Demerits:**
  - o **Time-Consuming:**
    - Example: Inquiry-based learning can be time-consuming, potentially limiting content coverage.
  - o **Resource-Intensive:**
    - Example: Providing resources for investigations, such as lab equipment and research materials, can be costly.
  - o **Variable Outcomes:**
    - Example: Learning outcomes may vary based on individual student investigations and questions.
  - o **Assessment Challenges:**
    - Example: Assessing inquiry-based learning can be subjective and dependent on individual student work.

Classroom Scenarios:

1. **Science Class on Ecosystems:**
   - Students investigate the impact of different pollutants on local ecosystems, conducting experiments and presenting their findings.

2. **History Class on Ancient Civilizations:**
   - Students research different aspects of ancient civilizations, such as their culture, technology, and political systems, and present their findings.

3. **Math Class on Real-World Applications:**
   - Students formulate questions about the application of mathematical concepts in real-world scenarios, such as architecture or finance, and conduct research.

4. **Literature Class on Author Studies:**
   - Students investigate the life and works of different authors, analyzing their themes and writing styles, and presenting their research.

5. **Environmental Science Class on Climate Change:**
   - Students research the effects of climate change on different ecosystems, conducting experiments and presenting their findings.

8. Problem based Learning

Meaning: Problem-based learning (PBL) is a student-centered approach where students learn by solving complex, real-world problems. It involves collaboration, research, and critical thinking.

Purpose:

- To develop problem-solving, research, and collaboration skills.
- To apply theoretical knowledge to practical situations.

Steps with Examples:

1. **Problem Introduction:**
   - Example: In a healthcare class, students are presented with a case of a patient with multiple health issues.

2. **Problem Analysis:**
   - Example: Students analyze the patient's symptoms, medical history, and test results to identify the underlying issues.

3. **Research:**
   - Example: Students conduct research on potential diagnoses and treatments, consulting medical literature and resources.

4. **Solution Development:**

   o Example: Students develop a treatment plan for the patient, considering different options and their implications.

5. **Presentation and Reflection:**

   o Example: Students present their treatment plan to the class, discussing their reasoning and reflecting on the learning process.

Criteria:

- Real-world, complex problems.
- Collaborative group work.
- Research and critical thinking.
- Clear connections to curriculum objectives.

Role of Teacher with Classroom Examples:

- **Facilitator:**

  o Example: The teacher facilitates group work, guiding students in their problem analysis and research.

- **Resource Provider:**

  o Example: The teacher provides resources, such as medical literature and case studies, to support student research.

- **Mentor:**
  - o Example: The teacher mentors students throughout their problem-solving process, providing feedback and support.
- **Evaluator:**
  - o Example: The teacher assesses student solutions and presentations based on their problem-solving methods and reasoning.

Merits and Demerits with Examples:

- **Merits:**
  - o **Real-World Application:**
    - Example: Solving a patient case helps students apply medical knowledge to real-world scenarios.
  - o **Skill Development:**
    - Example: PBL develops problem-solving, research, and collaboration skills.
  - o **Engagement:**
    - Example: Real-world problems engage students and make learning more relevant and interesting.
  - o **Critical Thinking:**
    - Example: Analyzing complex problems fosters critical thinking and decision-making skills.

- **Demerits:**
  - **Time-Consuming:**
    - Example: Solving complex problems can be time-consuming, potentially limiting content coverage.
  - **Resource-Intensive:**
    - Example: Providing resources for research and problem-solving can be costly.
  - **Variable Outcomes:**
    - Example: Learning outcomes may vary based on individual student group work and research.
  - **Assessment Challenges:**
    - Example: Assessing problem-based learning can be subjective and dependent on individual student work.

Classroom Scenarios:

1. **Engineering Class on Structural Design:**
   - Students are presented with a problem of designing a bridge for a specific location, considering factors such as materials, costs, and environmental impact.
2. **Business Class on Market Expansion:**
   - Students are given a problem of expanding a company's market to a new region, analyzing market trends, competition, and potential strategies.

3. **Education Class on Curriculum Development:**
   - Students are tasked with developing a curriculum for a new educational program, considering student needs, learning objectives, and resources.

4. **Healthcare Class on Patient Care:**
   - Students are presented with a complex patient case, developing a care plan based on the patient's symptoms, medical history, and test results.

5. **Environmental Science Class on Conservation:**
   - Students are given a problem of developing a conservation plan for a local ecosystem, researching potential strategies and their implications.

9. Project based Learning

Meaning: Project-based learning (PBL) is a student-centered approach where students learn by actively engaging in real-world and meaningful projects. It involves research, collaboration, and the application of knowledge to create a tangible product or solution.

Purpose:

- To develop research, collaboration, and project management skills.
- To apply theoretical knowledge to practical projects.

Steps with Examples:

1. **Project Selection:**
   - Example: In a science class, students choose a project on renewable energy solutions for their community.
2. **Planning:**
   - Example: Students develop a project plan, outlining their goals, research methods, and timeline.

3. **Research and Implementation:**
   - Example: Students conduct research on different renewable energy sources, collecting data and designing their project.

4. **Creation:**
   - Example: Students create a prototype or model of their renewable energy solution, such as a solar panel or wind turbine.

5. **Presentation and Reflection:**
   - Example: Students present their project to the class, discussing their findings, challenges, and reflections on the learning process.

Criteria:

- Real-world, meaningful projects.
- Opportunities for research and collaboration.
- Application of knowledge to create a tangible product or solution.
- Clear connections to curriculum objectives.

Role of Teacher with Classroom Examples:

- **Facilitator:**
  - Example: The teacher facilitates project work, guiding students in their research and project development.

- **Resource Provider:**
  - Example: The teacher provides resources, such as research materials and project supplies, to support student projects.
- **Mentor:**
  - Example: The teacher mentors students throughout their project work, providing feedback and support.
- **Evaluator:**
  - Example: The teacher assesses student projects and presentations based on their research methods, product, and reflections.

Merits and Demerits with Examples:

- **Merits:**
  - **Real-World Application:**
    - Example: Creating a renewable energy solution helps students apply science concepts to real-world projects.
  - **Skill Development:**
    - Example: PBL develops research, collaboration, and project management skills.
  - **Engagement:**
    - Example: Meaningful projects engage students and make learning more relevant and interesting.

- o **Critical Thinking:**
  - Example: Planning and creating projects fosters critical thinking and problem-solving skills.

- **Demerits:**
  - o **Time-Consuming:**
    - Example: Developing and completing projects can be time-consuming, potentially limiting content coverage.
  - o **Resource-Intensive:**
    - Example: Providing resources for projects can be costly.
  - o **Variable Outcomes:**
    - Example: Learning outcomes may vary based on individual student projects and research.
  - o **Assessment Challenges:**
    - Example: Assessing project-based learning can be subjective and dependent on individual student work.

Classroom Scenarios:

1. **Engineering Class on Robotics:**
   - o Students design and build a robot for a specific task, such as navigating a maze or picking up objects.

2. **Art Class on Public Art:**
   - Students create a public art installation for their community, researching different art forms and materials.

3. **Business Class on Entrepreneurship:**
   - Students develop a business plan for a startup, researching market trends, competition, and potential strategies.

4. **Environmental Science Class on Sustainability:**
   - Students design a sustainable community garden, researching different plants, irrigation systems, and environmental impacts.

5. **History Class on Local History:**
   - Students create a documentary or exhibit on the local history of their community, researching historical events, people, and landmarks.

10. Scenario based Learning

Meaning: Scenario-Based Learning (SBL) is an instructional design model that uses real-life or hypothetical scenarios to engage learners in critical thinking and problem-solving. It immerses students in a realistic situation where they must apply their knowledge and skills to resolve a complex issue.

Definitions by Experts:

1. **Clark Aldrich**: "Scenario-based learning presents learners with stories where they can practice the application of knowledge and skills. These scenarios can simulate the complexity and dynamics of real-world situations."

2. **Gilly Salmon**: "Scenario-based learning is an instructional approach that provides learners with realistic scenarios in which they can engage in critical thinking and apply their knowledge in a practical context."

Purpose:

- **Engagement**: By presenting students with realistic scenarios, SBL captures their interest and motivates them to learn.

- o **Example**: A medical student might be given a scenario involving a patient with complex symptoms to diagnose and treat.
- **Critical Thinking**: SBL encourages learners to think critically and make decisions based on their understanding.
  - o **Example**: Business students may be presented with a scenario involving a company's financial crisis and asked to propose solutions.
- **Skill Application**: It helps learners apply theoretical knowledge to practical situations.
  - o **Example**: Law students might work through a legal case scenario to apply their knowledge of law principles.

Steps with Examples:

1. **Identify Learning Objectives**:
   - o Determine what skills or knowledge the scenario aims to teach.
   - o Example: For a nursing course, the objective might be to improve patient care skills.

2. **Create Realistic Scenarios**:
   - o Develop scenarios that are relevant and challenging.
   - o Example: A cybersecurity class might use a scenario where students must respond to a data breach.

3. **Present the Scenario**:
   - Introduce the scenario to students, providing all necessary background information.
   - Example: In an environmental science class, present a scenario about a community facing water contamination.

4. **Facilitate Discussion and Problem-Solving**:
   - Encourage students to discuss the scenario and explore different solutions.
   - Example: In a history class, students might debate various strategies a historical figure could have used.

5. **Debrief and Reflect**:
   - Review the outcomes and discuss what was learned.
   - Example: After resolving a marketing scenario, students reflect on the strategies they used and their effectiveness.

Criteria:

- **Relevance**: Scenarios should be relevant to the learners' experiences and learning objectives.
  - **Example**: In a criminal justice class, scenarios should relate to real-world law enforcement challenges.
- **Complexity**: Scenarios should be sufficiently complex to challenge students and promote critical thinking.

- o **Example**: In a project management course, scenarios could involve multiple stakeholders and conflicting priorities.
- **Realism**: Scenarios must be realistic to ensure learners can relate and engage with them.
  - o **Example**: Medical students might use scenarios based on actual patient cases.
- **Feedback**: Provide feedback during and after the scenario to enhance learning.
  - o **Example**: In a customer service training, feedback might be given on how well students handled a difficult customer.

Role of Teacher with Classroom Examples:

- **Facilitator**:
  - o Guide students through the scenario, encouraging discussion and reflection.
  - o Example: In a leadership training, the teacher facilitates a scenario where students must lead a team through a crisis.
- **Resource Provider**:
  - o Provide necessary resources and information to support students in resolving the scenario.
  - o Example: In a science class, provide data and research materials for a scenario on climate change.

- **Mentor**:
    - Offer support and feedback throughout the scenario-based activity.
    - Example: In a nursing course, mentor students as they navigate a patient care scenario.
- **Evaluator**:
    - Assess students' performance and provide constructive feedback.
    - Example: In a business ethics class, evaluate students' decision-making in a corporate scandal scenario.

Merits and Demerits with Examples:

- **Merits**:
    - **Engagement**:
        - Example: Students are more engaged when working through a scenario that feels relevant and real.
    - **Critical Thinking**:
        - Example: Scenarios require students to analyze information and make decisions, enhancing critical thinking skills.

- o **Real-World Application**:
  - Example: Applying theoretical knowledge to practical scenarios helps students see the relevance of their learning.
- o **Collaboration**:
  - Example: Working on scenarios in groups fosters teamwork and communication skills.

- **Demerits**:
  - o **Time-Consuming**:
    - Example: Developing and implementing scenarios can be time-consuming for teachers.
  - o **Resource-Intensive**:
    - Example: Realistic scenarios may require extensive resources, such as detailed background information or specialized materials.
  - o **Variable Outcomes**:
    - Example: Different students may arrive at different solutions, making assessment challenging.
  - o **Potential for Misalignment**:
    - Example: If scenarios are not well-aligned with learning objectives, they may not effectively teach the intended skills or knowledge.

Classroom Scenarios:

1. **Medical Diagnosis Scenario**:
   - Students diagnose and treat a patient with multiple symptoms, practicing their clinical decision-making skills.

2. **Environmental Crisis Scenario**:
   - Environmental science students develop a response plan for a community facing water contamination.

3. **Corporate Ethics Scenario**:
   - Business students address an ethical dilemma within a fictional company, exploring the implications of different decisions.

4. **Historical Decision-Making Scenario**:
   - History students role-play as advisors to a historical figure, debating and deciding on a course of action during a critical event.

5. **Cybersecurity Breach Scenario**:
   - Cybersecurity students respond to a simulated data breach, identifying vulnerabilities and proposing solutions.

11. Role Play / Dramatization

Meaning: Role play or dramatization involves students acting out roles in specific scenarios to explore complex issues, develop empathy, and practice communication and problem-solving skills.

Definitions by Experts:

1. **Dorothy Heathcote**: "Role play is a method in which students assume roles and act out scenarios, allowing them to explore real-life situations and develop a deeper understanding of the content."

2. **Gavin Bolton**: "Dramatization in education is a process-oriented method that uses the art of theatre to facilitate learning, encouraging students to engage with the material in a dynamic and interactive way."

Purpose:

- **Develop Empathy**: Role play helps students understand different perspectives and develop empathy.
  - **Example**: In a social studies class, students role-play as historical figures to understand their motivations and challenges.
- **Enhance Communication Skills**: It promotes effective communication and interpersonal skills.

- o **Example**: In a language arts class, students dramatize a scene from a play to practice expressive language and dialogue.
- **Promote Critical Thinking**: Role play encourages students to think critically about complex issues.
  - o **Example**: In a science class, students role-play as environmental activists and corporate representatives debating a pollution issue.

Steps with Examples:

1. **Introduce the Scenario**:
   - o Present the context and roles to the students.
   - o Example: In a history class, introduce a scenario where students role-play as delegates at a peace conference.

2. **Assign Roles**:
   - o Assign specific roles to students, ensuring a balance of perspectives.
   - o Example: In a literature class, assign roles of different characters in a novel.

3. **Prepare and Rehearse**:
   - o Allow students time to prepare and rehearse their roles.
   - o Example: In a drama class, students rehearse a scene from a Shakespeare play.

4. **Perform**:

   o Students act out the scenario, staying in character.

   o Example: In a health education class, students role-play a doctor-patient consultation.

5. **Debrief and Reflect**:

   o Discuss the performance and reflect on the learning outcomes.

   o Example: In a psychology class, debrief after a role play about a therapy session, discussing different approaches and their effectiveness.

Criteria:

- **Relevance**: Ensure the roles and scenarios are relevant to the learning objectives.

  o **Example**: In a government class, role plays should reflect real political processes and debates.

- **Engagement**: Scenarios should be engaging and interesting to students.

  o **Example**: In a language class, choose culturally relevant and interesting scenarios for role play.

- **Balance**: Assign roles to ensure a balanced representation of perspectives.

  o **Example**: In a sociology class, assign roles to reflect different social groups in a community issue.

- **Guidance**: Provide clear guidance and support to students throughout the process.
  - o **Example**: In a business class, guide students in preparing for a role play about a board meeting.

Role of Teacher with Classroom Examples:

- **Facilitator**:
  - o Guide students through the role play process, ensuring they understand their roles and the scenario.
  - o Example: In a political science class, facilitate a mock election role play.
- **Director**:
  - o Act as a director, helping students to rehearse and refine their performances.
  - o Example: In a theatre class, direct students in a scene from a play.
- **Mentor**:
  - o Mentor students, providing feedback and support during rehearsals and performances.
  - o Example: In a leadership training, mentor students role-playing different leadership styles.
- **Evaluator**:
  - o Assess student performances and provide constructive feedback.
  - o Example: In a communication class, evaluate students' role play of a conflict resolution scenario.

Merits and Demerits with Examples:

- **Merits**:
  - **Engagement**:
    - Example: Students are more engaged when actively participating in a role play about a current event.
  - **Empathy Development**:
    - Example: Role play helps students understand different perspectives, such as playing the role of different stakeholders in a community issue.
  - **Communication Skills**:
    - Example: Acting out scenarios enhances students' verbal and non-verbal communication skills.
  - **Critical Thinking**:
    - Example: Role play scenarios require students to think on their feet and make decisions based on their roles.
- **Demerits**:
  - **Time-Consuming**:
    - Example: Preparing and rehearsing for role plays can be time-consuming.

- o **Resource-Intensive**:
    - Example: Effective role plays may require props, costumes, or additional materials.
- o **Potential for Discomfort**:
    - Example: Some students may feel uncomfortable or self-conscious acting in front of their peers.
- o **Variable Engagement**:
    - Example: Not all students may be equally engaged, especially if they do not find the roles or scenarios relevant or interesting.

Classroom Scenarios:

1. **Historical Debate Role Play**:
   - o Students role-play as historical figures debating a significant event, such as the signing of the Declaration of Independence.

2. **Customer Service Scenario**:
   - o Business students role-play customer service representatives handling difficult customers.

3. **Therapy Session Role Play**:
   - o Psychology students role-play a therapist and client in a counseling session.

4. **Courtroom Drama**:

   o Law students role-play a courtroom trial, with roles such as judge, lawyers, and witnesses.

5. **Cultural Exchange Role Play**:

   o Language students role-play a cultural exchange scenario, practicing language skills and cultural understanding.

12. Simulation

Meaning: Simulation is a teaching method that creates a virtual environment in which students can interact, make decisions, and experience the outcomes of their actions in a controlled, risk-free setting.

Definitions by Experts:

1. **David Kolb**: "Simulation is an experiential learning method that provides learners with opportunities to engage in realistic, interactive environments where they can apply their knowledge and skills."
2. **Donald Schön**: "Simulation involves the creation of complex, dynamic models that replicate real-world scenarios, allowing learners to experiment and learn from the outcomes."

Purpose:

- **Risk-Free Learning**: Allows students to make decisions and learn from mistakes without real-world consequences.
  - **Example**: Medical students practice surgical procedures using simulation technology without risking patient safety.

- **Real-World Application**: Helps students apply theoretical knowledge in practical scenarios.
  - o **Example**: Business students use simulation software to manage a virtual company and make strategic decisions.
- **Skill Development**: Enhances practical and decision-making skills through hands-on experience.
  - o **Example**: Engineering students use flight simulators to learn about aircraft operations.

Steps with Examples:

1. **Define Learning Objectives**:
   - o Identify the skills and knowledge the simulation aims to teach.
   - o Example: In a nursing program, the objective might be to practice emergency response protocols.

2. **Develop or Select a Simulation**:
   - o Create or choose a simulation that accurately represents the desired scenario.
   - o Example: A flight school selects a flight simulator for pilot training.

3. **Introduce the Simulation**:
   - o Explain the simulation's purpose, rules, and objectives to the students.

o Example: In a business class, introduce a market simulation where students manage a virtual company.

4. **Facilitate the Simulation**:
   o Guide students through the simulation, providing support as needed.
   o Example: In a computer science class, facilitate a coding simulation where students troubleshoot software bugs.

5. **Debrief and Reflect**:
   o Review the simulation outcomes and discuss what was learned.
   o Example: After a medical simulation, debrief with students about their decision-making and patient care.

Criteria:

- **Realism**: Simulations should accurately reflect real-world scenarios.
   o **Example**: In a military training program, simulations should mimic real combat conditions.
- **Interactivity**: Ensure the simulation allows for active student participation and decision-making.
   o **Example**: In a finance course, use a stock market simulation where students can buy and sell stocks.

- **Feedback**: Provide immediate feedback to help students understand the consequences of their actions.
    - o **Example**: In a flight simulation, provide real-time feedback on flight performance.
- **Relevance**: The simulation should align with the learning objectives and course content.
    - o **Example**: In a medical training program, use simulations relevant to the specific medical procedures being taught.

Role of Teacher with Classroom Examples:

- **Facilitator**:
    - o Guide students through the simulation, ensuring they understand the objectives and process.
    - o Example: In a business simulation, guide students as they manage their virtual companies.
- **Supporter**:
    - o Provide support and resources to help students navigate the simulation.
    - o Example: In a cybersecurity simulation, provide resources and support as students respond to a simulated cyberattack.
- **Evaluator**:
    - o Assess student performance and provide feedback on their decisions and actions.

- o Example: In a medical simulation, evaluate students' performance in diagnosing and treating virtual patients.
- **Debrief Leader**:
  - o Lead debriefing sessions to discuss the outcomes and learning points from the simulation.
  - o Example: After a flight simulation, lead a debrief to discuss flight maneuvers and decision-making.

Merits and Demerits with Examples:

- **Merits**:
  - o **Risk-Free Environment**:
    - Example: Medical simulations allow students to practice procedures without risking patient safety.
  - o **Real-World Experience**:
    - Example: Business simulations provide experience in managing a company and making strategic decisions.
  - o **Immediate Feedback**:
    - Example: Flight simulators provide real-time feedback on flight performance.
  - o **Enhanced Engagement**:
    - Example: Interactive simulations engage students and make learning more dynamic.

- **Demerits**:
  - **Resource-Intensive**:
    - Example: High-quality simulations can be expensive and require significant resources.
  - **Complexity**:
    - Example: Complex simulations may be challenging for some students to navigate and understand.
  - **Technical Issues**:
    - Example: Simulations relying on technology can face technical glitches and interruptions.
  - **Potential for Misalignment**:
    - Example: If not well-designed, simulations may not effectively teach the intended skills or knowledge.

Classroom Scenarios:

1. **Medical Emergency Simulation**:
   - Nursing students practice responding to a simulated cardiac arrest situation.
2. **Business Strategy Simulation**:
   - Business students manage a virtual company, making decisions on marketing, finance, and operations.

3. **Environmental Impact Simulation**:

   o Environmental science students use a simulation to explore the impact of different policies on climate change.

4. **Stock Market Simulation**:

   o Finance students participate in a simulated stock market, buying and selling stocks to learn about market dynamics.

5. **Flight Training Simulation**:

   o Aviation students use flight simulators to practice take-offs, landings, and emergency procedures.

13. Field Work/Onsite Learning

Meaning: Field work or onsite learning involves taking students out of the classroom to engage in learning activities in real-world settings, allowing them to apply theoretical knowledge in practical contexts.

Definitions by Experts:

1. **John Dewey**: "Field work provides an opportunity for students to engage in experiential learning, connecting classroom theory with real-world practice."

2. **Kurt Lewin**: "Onsite learning is a method that immerses students in real-world environments, allowing them to observe, interact, and learn from their experiences."

Purpose:

- **Practical Application**: Helps students apply classroom knowledge to real-world situations.
  - **Example**: Geography students conduct fieldwork to study local landforms and ecosystems.
- **Experiential Learning**: Enhances learning through direct experience and observation.
  - **Example**: Biology students visit a nature reserve to study plant and animal species.

- **Engagement and Motivation**: Engages students by providing hands-on learning experiences.
  - o **Example**: History students visit a historical site to learn about its significance firsthand.

Steps with Examples:

1. **Plan and Prepare**:
   - o Identify learning objectives and plan the fieldwork activities.
   - o Example: In a geology class, plan a field trip to a local rock formation to study geological processes.

2. **Brief Students**:
   - o Provide students with background information and guidelines for the fieldwork.
   - o Example: In a sociology class, brief students on the community they will be studying and the research methods they will use.

3. **Conduct Fieldwork**:
   - o Take students to the field site and guide them through the activities.
   - o Example: In an environmental science class, conduct fieldwork at a wetland to study water quality and biodiversity.

4. **Collect Data and Observations**:
   - o Have students collect data, make observations, and take notes during the fieldwork.

- o Example: In an archaeology class, students collect artifacts and record their findings at a dig site.

5. **Debrief and Reflect**:
   - o Discuss the fieldwork experience and reflect on the learning outcomes.
   - o Example: In an urban studies class, debrief after a city tour to discuss urban planning and development.

Criteria:

- **Relevance**: Fieldwork activities should be directly related to the learning objectives and course content.
  - o **Example**: In a marine biology class, fieldwork should focus on marine ecosystems and species.
- **Preparation**: Ensure students are well-prepared and understand the objectives and guidelines.
  - o **Example**: In an anthropology class, provide students with research methods and safety guidelines for fieldwork.
- **Supervision**: Provide adequate supervision to ensure safety and support during fieldwork.
  - o **Example**: In an environmental science class, have sufficient staff to supervise students during fieldwork at a nature reserve.
- **Reflection**: Include opportunities for students to reflect on their experiences and connect them to classroom learning.

- o **Example**: In a history class, have students write reflective essays after visiting a historical site.

Role of Teacher with Classroom Examples:

- **Planner**:
  - o Plan and organize the fieldwork, ensuring it aligns with learning objectives.
  - o Example: In a geology class, plan a field trip to study rock formations and geological processes.

- **Guide**:
  - o Guide students through the fieldwork activities, providing support and supervision.
  - o Example: In a biology class, guide students as they conduct fieldwork at a nature reserve.

- **Facilitator**:
  - o Facilitate data collection and observations, helping students to stay focused and organized.
  - o Example: In a sociology class, facilitate students' observations and interviews in a community study.

- **Debrief Leader**:
  - o Lead debriefing sessions to discuss the fieldwork experience and learning outcomes.
  - o Example: In an urban studies class, lead a debrief after a city tour to discuss urban planning and development.

Merits and Demerits with Examples:

- **Merits**:
  - **Hands-On Learning**:
    - Example: Students gain practical experience by conducting fieldwork in real-world settings.
  - **Enhanced Engagement**:
    - Example: Fieldwork activities are engaging and motivating for students.
  - **Real-World Application**:
    - Example: Students apply classroom knowledge to real-world situations, enhancing their understanding.
  - **Skill Development**:
    - Example: Fieldwork helps students develop research, observation, and data collection skills.
- **Demerits**:
  - **Logistical Challenges**:
    - Example: Organizing field trips can be challenging due to transportation, permissions, and scheduling.

- o **Safety Concerns**:
  - Example: Fieldwork in certain environments may pose safety risks that need to be managed.
- o **Resource-Intensive**:
  - Example: Fieldwork may require significant resources, such as funding, equipment, and supervision.
- o **Variable Learning Outcomes**:
  - Example: Learning outcomes from fieldwork may vary depending on the quality of the experience and student engagement.

Classroom Scenarios:

1. **Geology Field Trip**:
   - o Geology students visit a local rock formation to study geological processes and collect rock samples.
2. **Urban Studies Tour**:
   - o Urban studies students take a guided tour of a city to learn about urban planning and development.
3. **Environmental Science Fieldwork**:
   - o Environmental science students conduct fieldwork at a wetland to study water quality and biodiversity.

4. **Historical Site Visit**:

- o History students visit a historical site to learn about its significance and collect data for a research project.

5. **Community Sociology Study**:

- o Sociology students conduct fieldwork in a local community, observing and interviewing residents to study social dynamics.

14. Seminar method

Meaning: The seminar method is a teaching approach that involves structured group discussions and presentations on specific topics, encouraging active participation, critical thinking, and collaborative learning.

Definitions by Experts:

1. **Mortimer Adler**: "A seminar is a form of academic instruction that brings together a small group of students for interactive discussion and in-depth exploration of a topic."
2. **Parker Palmer**: "The seminar method fosters a community of inquiry where students engage in dialogue, share perspectives, and collaboratively build understanding."

Purpose:

- **Critical Thinking**: Encourages students to think deeply about complex issues and develop well-reasoned arguments.
  - **Example**: In a philosophy class, students discuss ethical dilemmas and develop arguments for different viewpoints.
- **Active Participation**: Promotes active participation and engagement in the learning process.
  - **Example**: In a literature class, students present and discuss their interpretations of a novel.

- **Collaborative Learning**: Facilitates collaborative learning and the sharing of diverse perspectives.
  - **Example**: In a political science class, students discuss different political theories and their implications.

Steps with Examples:

1. **Select a Topic**:
   - Choose a relevant and challenging topic for the seminar.
   - Example: In a history class, select a topic on the causes and consequences of the Industrial Revolution.

2. **Prepare Materials**:
   - Provide students with reading materials and resources to prepare for the seminar.
   - Example: In a sociology class, provide articles and case studies on social inequality.

3. **Assign Roles**:
   - Assign roles to students, such as presenters, discussants, and note-takers.
   - Example: In an economics class, assign students to present on different economic theories.

4. **Conduct the Seminar**:
   - Facilitate the seminar, ensuring all students have the opportunity to participate and contribute.

- o Example: In a psychology class, conduct a seminar on different approaches to psychotherapy.

5. **Debrief and Reflect**:
   - o Discuss the seminar outcomes and reflect on the learning experience.
   - o Example: In a political science class, debrief after a seminar on international relations theories.

Criteria:

- **Relevance**: Ensure the seminar topic is relevant to the course content and learning objectives.
  - o **Example**: In a history class, select seminar topics related to key historical events and themes.
- **Preparation**: Provide students with adequate resources and time to prepare for the seminar.
  - o **Example**: In a literature class, provide students with reading materials and questions to guide their preparation.
- **Participation**: Encourage active participation and ensure all students have the opportunity to contribute.
  - o **Example**: In a sociology class, create a seminar format that allows for small group discussions and presentations.
- **Guidance**: Provide clear guidelines and support to help students prepare and participate effectively.

- o **Example**: In a philosophy class, provide guidelines on how to structure arguments and engage in critical discussions.

Role of Teacher with Classroom Examples:

- **Facilitator**:
  - o Facilitate the seminar, ensuring balanced participation and guiding the discussion.
  - o Example: In a political science class, facilitate a seminar on different forms of government.

- **Resource Provider**:
  - o Provide students with resources and support to help them prepare for the seminar.
  - o Example: In a history class, provide primary source documents for students to analyze and discuss.

- **Moderator**:
  - o Moderate the discussion, ensuring it stays on track and remains respectful.
  - o Example: In a sociology class, moderate a seminar on social justice issues.

- **Evaluator**:
  - o Assess student participation and contributions to the seminar.
  - o Example: In a literature class, evaluate students' presentations and discussions on a novel.

Merits and Demerits with Examples:

- **Merits**:
  - **Critical Thinking**:
    - Example: Students develop critical thinking skills by engaging in in-depth discussions and analysis.
  - **Active Participation**:
    - Example: The seminar format encourages all students to actively participate and contribute.
  - **Collaborative Learning**:
    - Example: Students learn from each other by sharing diverse perspectives and insights.
  - **Communication Skills**:
    - Example: Presenting and discussing in a seminar enhances students' verbal communication skills.
- **Demerits**:
  - **Time-Consuming**:
    - Example: Preparing for and conducting seminars can be time-consuming for both teachers and students.

- o **Variable Participation**:
  - Example: Not all students may participate equally, and some may dominate the discussion.
- o **Resource-Intensive**:
  - Example: Effective seminars require extensive reading materials and preparation.
- o **Potential for Off-Topic Discussions**:
  - Example: Discussions can sometimes veer off-topic, requiring careful moderation.

Classroom Scenarios:

1. **Philosophy Seminar**:
   - o Philosophy students discuss and debate ethical dilemmas, presenting different arguments and perspectives.
2. **Literature Analysis Seminar**:
   - o Literature students present and discuss their interpretations of a novel, exploring themes and characters.
3. **Political Science Seminar**:
   - o Political science students discuss different political theories and their implications for governance.

4. **Sociology Seminar**:

   o Sociology students discuss social inequality, presenting case studies and research findings.

5. **History Seminar**:

   o History students discuss the causes and consequences of the Industrial Revolution, using primary sources and historical analysis.

15. Demonstration Method

Meaning: The demonstration method involves showing students how to do something through a step-by-step process, allowing them to observe and understand the procedure before trying it themselves.

Definitions by Experts:

1. **Albert Bandura**: "Demonstration is a method of teaching that involves showing students how to perform a task or procedure, allowing them to learn through observation and imitation."

2. **Jean Piaget**: "The demonstration method provides a concrete and practical way for students to understand abstract concepts by observing and engaging in hands-on activities."

Purpose:

- **Visual Learning**: Helps students understand procedures and concepts through visual demonstration.
  - **Example**: In a chemistry class, demonstrating a chemical reaction helps students understand the process and safety precautions.
- **Skill Development**: Allows students to learn and practice skills by observing and imitating.

- o **Example**: In a cooking class, demonstrating a cooking technique helps students learn how to prepare a dish.
- **Immediate Feedback**: Provides opportunities for immediate feedback and correction.
  - o **Example**: In a woodworking class, demonstrating the use of tools allows the teacher to provide immediate feedback on technique and safety.

Steps with Examples:

1. **Preparation**:
   - o Plan the demonstration, gather materials, and ensure all necessary equipment is ready.
   - o Example: In a biology class, prepare specimens and equipment for a dissection demonstration.

2. **Introduction**:
   - o Introduce the demonstration, explaining its purpose and relevance to the students.
   - o Example: In a physics class, introduce a demonstration on the principles of motion and force.

3. **Conduct the Demonstration**:
   - o Perform the demonstration, clearly explaining each step and its significance.
   - o Example: In a chemistry class, conduct a demonstration of a titration experiment, explaining each step and its importance.

4. **Student Observation and Questions**:

    o Encourage students to observe closely and ask questions during the demonstration.

    o Example: In an art class, demonstrate a painting technique and invite students to ask questions about the process.

5. **Student Practice**:

    o Allow students to practice the demonstrated procedure under supervision.

    o Example: In a culinary class, students practice the demonstrated cooking technique, with the teacher providing guidance and feedback.

6. **Review and Reflect**:

    o Review the demonstration and its outcomes, discussing what was learned and addressing any questions.

    o Example: In a robotics class, review the demonstrated programming technique and discuss the outcomes with students.

Criteria:

- **Clarity**: Ensure the demonstration is clear and easy to follow, with step-by-step explanations.

    o **Example**: In a chemistry class, clearly explain each step of a chemical reaction demonstration.

- **Relevance**: The demonstration should be directly related to the learning objectives and course content.
  - o **Example**: In a physics class, demonstrate experiments that illustrate key principles being studied.
- **Engagement**: Engage students by encouraging observation, questions, and participation.
  - o **Example**: In a biology class, engage students by encouraging them to ask questions during a dissection demonstration.
- **Safety**: Ensure all safety precautions are followed during the demonstration.
  - o **Example**: In a woodworking class, demonstrate the safe use of tools and equipment.

Role of Teacher with Classroom Examples:

- **Planner**:
  - o Plan and organize the demonstration, ensuring all materials and equipment are ready.
  - o Example: In a chemistry class, prepare all chemicals and equipment for a demonstration of a chemical reaction.
- **Presenter**:
  - o Conduct the demonstration, clearly explaining each step and its significance.

- o Example: In a cooking class, demonstrate a cooking technique, explaining each step in detail.

- **Facilitator**:
  - o Facilitate student observation and questions, encouraging active participation.
  - o Example: In an art class, facilitate questions and discussions during a demonstration of a painting technique.

- **Supervisor**:
  - o Supervise students as they practice the demonstrated procedure, providing guidance and feedback.
  - o Example: In a robotics class, supervise students as they practice programming techniques demonstrated in class.

Merits and Demerits with Examples:

- **Merits**:
  - o **Visual Learning**:
    - Example: Students understand procedures better by seeing them demonstrated.
  - o **Immediate Feedback**:
    - Example: Teachers can provide immediate feedback and correction during student practice.

- o **Hands-On Learning**:
  - Example: Students engage in hands-on learning by practicing demonstrated procedures.
- o **Skill Development**:
  - Example: Demonstrations help students develop practical skills through observation and practice.
- **Demerits**:
  - o **Time-Consuming**:
    - Example: Demonstrations can be time-consuming, especially if they involve complex procedures.
  - o **Resource-Intensive**:
    - Example: Demonstrations may require significant resources, such as materials and equipment.
  - o **Variable Understanding**:
    - Example: Not all students may understand the demonstration equally, requiring additional explanation and support.
  - o **Safety Concerns**:
    - Example: Some demonstrations, especially in science and technical subjects, may involve safety risks that need to be managed.

Classroom Scenarios:

1. **Chemistry Experiment Demonstration**:
   - Chemistry students observe a demonstration of a chemical reaction, learning about the process and safety precautions.

2. **Cooking Technique Demonstration**:
   - Culinary students watch a demonstration of a cooking technique, then practice it under supervision.

3. **Art Technique Demonstration**:
   - Art students observe a demonstration of a painting or drawing technique, then try it themselves.

4. **Woodworking Tool Use Demonstration**:
   - Woodworking students watch a demonstration of how to use tools safely and effectively, then practice using them.

5. **Robotics Programming Demonstration**:
   - Robotics students observe a demonstration of programming techniques, then practice coding and testing their own programs.

16. Scaffolding Method

Meaning: Scaffolding is a teaching method that involves providing students with temporary support structures to aid their learning process. These supports are gradually removed as students develop the necessary skills and knowledge to perform tasks independently.

Definitions by Experts:

1. **Lev Vygotsky**: "Scaffolding is the process by which a teacher or more knowledgeable other provides temporary support to students to help them accomplish a task they cannot complete independently."

2. **Jerome Bruner**: "Scaffolding involves the instructor providing successive levels of temporary support that help students achieve higher levels of comprehension and skill acquisition."

Purpose:

- **Enhance Learning**: Helps students understand complex concepts and perform tasks they might not be able to do on their own.
  - o **Example**: In a math class, a teacher provides step-by-step guidance on solving algebraic equations, gradually reducing help as students become more proficient.

- **Build Independence**: Encourages students to become independent learners by gradually removing supports.
  - o **Example**: In a writing class, a teacher initially provides sentence starters and outlines, then gradually encourages students to write more independently.
- **Bridge Knowledge Gaps**: Addresses gaps in students' knowledge and skills by providing targeted support.
  - o **Example**: In a science class, a teacher helps students understand complex scientific concepts through simplified explanations and visual aids.

Steps with Examples:

1. **Assess Student Needs**:
   - o Determine the areas where students need support.
   - o Example: In a language class, assess students' proficiency in grammar and vocabulary to identify areas for scaffolding.

2. **Provide Support**:
   - o Offer appropriate support structures, such as hints, prompts, and modeling.
   - o Example: In a history class, provide a timeline of events to help students understand the sequence of historical events.

3. **Gradually Remove Support**:

- o Reduce the level of support as students gain confidence and competence.
- o Example: In a math class, initially provide worked examples, then gradually reduce the number of steps shown.

4. **Encourage Independent Practice**:
   - o Encourage students to practice independently, using the skills and knowledge they have developed.
   - o Example: In a science class, after guided experiments, encourage students to design and conduct their own experiments.

5. **Monitor and Adjust**:
   - o Monitor student progress and adjust support as needed to ensure continued learning.
   - o Example: In a literature class, provide feedback on students' essays and adjust guidance based on their progress.

Criteria:

- **Student Readiness**: Ensure scaffolding is tailored to the current skill level and readiness of the students.
  - o **Example**: In a foreign language class, provide more scaffolding for beginner students and less for advanced students.
- **Flexibility**: Be flexible in the level and type of support provided, adjusting based on student needs.

- o **Example**: In a math class, adjust the amount of guidance based on students' performance on practice problems.
- **Clear Objectives**: Have clear learning objectives that the scaffolding aims to achieve.
  - o **Example**: In a history class, clearly define the goal of understanding the causes and effects of a historical event.
- **Gradual Removal**: Plan for the gradual removal of supports to promote independence.
  - o **Example**: In a writing class, start with detailed outlines and gradually move to independent writing assignments.

Role of Teacher with Classroom Examples:

- **Diagnostician**:
  - o Assess student needs and identify areas for scaffolding.
  - o Example: In a math class, diagnose students' understanding of algebraic concepts to determine where support is needed.
- **Guide**:
  - o Provide guidance and support through modeling and explanations.
  - o Example: In a science class, guide students through a complex experiment by demonstrating each step.

- **Facilitator**:
  - Facilitate learning by offering hints and prompts without providing direct answers.
  - Example: In a literature class, facilitate a discussion by prompting students with guiding questions.
- **Evaluator**:
  - Monitor student progress and adjust scaffolding based on their development.
  - Example: In a history class, evaluate students' understanding through formative assessments and adjust support accordingly.

Merits and Demerits with Examples:

- **Merits**:
  - **Enhanced Understanding**:
    - Example: Students develop a deeper understanding of complex concepts through guided learning.
  - **Skill Development**:
    - Example: Scaffolding helps students develop critical thinking and problem-solving skills by gradually increasing task complexity.
  - **Promotes Independence**:
    - Example: Students become more independent learners as supports are gradually removed.

- o **Addresses Individual Needs**:
  - ▪ Example: Tailored scaffolding meets the specific needs of each student, improving learning outcomes.

- **Demerits**:
  - o **Time-Consuming**:
    - ▪ Example: Providing individualized scaffolding can be time-consuming for teachers.
  - o **Over-Dependence**:
    - ▪ Example: Some students may become overly dependent on scaffolding and struggle when it is removed.
  - o **Inconsistent Application**:
    - ▪ Example: Inconsistent or inadequate scaffolding can lead to gaps in learning.
  - o **Resource-Intensive**:
    - ▪ Example: Effective scaffolding may require significant resources, such as additional materials and time for planning.

Classroom Scenarios:

1. **Math Problem Solving**:
   - o Math students are given a complex algebra problem. The teacher provides step-by-step guidance initially

and gradually reduces help as students practice independently.

2. **Science Experiment Design**:
   - Science students are tasked with designing an experiment. The teacher models the process and provides prompts, gradually allowing students to take more control.

3. **History Research Project**:
   - History students undertake a research project. The teacher provides initial research questions and sources, then encourages students to find and analyze additional sources independently.

4. **Language Learning**:
   - Language students learn new grammar rules. The teacher provides sentence structures and examples, then gradually encourages students to create their own sentences using the rules.

17. Group Work / Participative Method

Meaning: Group work, also known as participative or collaborative learning, involves students working together in small groups to achieve a common goal. It emphasizes active participation, cooperation, and shared responsibility.

Definitions by Experts:

1. **Johnson, Johnson, and Smith (1998)**: "Cooperative learning is the instructional use of small groups so that students work together to maximize their own and each other's learning."
2. **Slavin (1996)**: "Collaborative learning is a situation in which two or more people learn or attempt to learn something together."

Purpose

- **Enhances Learning**: Encourages active engagement and deeper understanding through discussion and peer teaching.
- **Develops Social Skills**: Promotes communication, teamwork, and conflict resolution skills.
- **Increases Motivation**: Students are often more motivated to learn when working with peers.

- **Promotes Critical Thinking**: Diverse perspectives lead to more critical and creative thinking.

Example: In a history class, students might work in groups to analyze different primary sources from World War II and present their findings to the class.

Steps

1. **Form Groups**: Divide students into small, diverse groups.
2. **Assign Tasks**: Clearly define the task or project for each group.
3. **Set Guidelines**: Establish rules and expectations for group work.
4. **Monitor Progress**: Teacher circulates to provide guidance and support.
5. **Presentation**: Groups present their work to the class.
6. **Assessment**: Evaluate both the group product and individual contributions.

Example: In a science class, groups might conduct experiments and then share their results with the class.

Criteria

- **Clear Objectives**: The task should have clear and achievable goals.

- **Group Composition**: Groups should be diverse in terms of abilities and backgrounds.
- **Defined Roles**: Assign specific roles to each group member to ensure participation.
- **Assessment Methods**: Use a mix of group and individual assessments.

Example: In a literature class, roles might include a summarizer, a questioner, and a connector who relates the text to other knowledge.

Role of Teacher

- **Facilitator**: Guides the groups, provides resources, and helps resolve conflicts.
- **Evaluator**: Assesses both the process and the final product.
- **Motivator**: Encourages participation and ensures all voices are heard.

Classroom Example: In a math class, the teacher might help a group struggling with a problem by asking guiding questions rather than providing answers.

Merits and Demerits

Merits:

- **Enhanced Engagement**: Active participation increases interest and motivation.

- **Development of Soft Skills**: Builds teamwork, communication, and leadership skills.
- **Diverse Perspectives**: Exposure to different viewpoints enhances learning.

Example: In an art class, group projects might lead to more creative outcomes than individual work.

Demerits:

- **Unequal Participation**: Some students may dominate while others may not contribute.
- **Group Conflicts**: Disagreements can hinder progress.
- **Assessment Challenges**: Difficult to assess individual contributions accurately.

Example: In a project-based learning environment, a few students might end up doing most of the work.

Classroom Scenarios:

Scenario 1: Science Project

- Students are divided into small groups to work on a science project about renewable energy sources. Each group must research a different type of renewable energy and present their findings to the class.

Scenario 2: Literature Circle

- In a literature class, students form groups to discuss a novel. Each member of the group has a specific role, such as summarizer, questioner, and connector. They then share their insights with the whole class.

Scenario 3: History Debate

- In a history class, students are divided into groups to debate different perspectives on a historical event. Each group must prepare arguments and counterarguments for their assigned perspective.

Scenario 4: Math Problem-Solving

- Students work in groups to solve a complex math problem. Each group must come up with a solution and explain their reasoning to the class, encouraging collaborative problem-solving and critical thinking.

Scenario 5: Art Collaborative Project

- In an art class, students collaborate on a large mural. Each group is responsible for a different section, but they must ensure their sections blend seamlessly with the others to create a cohesive final piece.

18. Tutorial Method

Meaning: The tutorial method involves personalized, one-on-one or small group instruction focused on the specific needs of the student(s). It is highly interactive and tailored to individual learning styles and paces.

Definitions by Experts:

1. **Vygotsky (1978)**: "Tutoring leverages the zone of proximal development by providing support that enables the learner to perform tasks they cannot do alone."
2. **Bruner (1966)**: "A tutorial system of education provides the means whereby the instructor can focus specifically on the needs of individual students."

Purpose

- **Personalized Learning**: Tailors instruction to the unique needs and pace of each student.
- **Targeted Support**: Focuses on specific areas where the student needs improvement.
- **Immediate Feedback**: Provides direct and immediate feedback to correct misunderstandings.
- **Building Confidence**: Helps build student confidence by providing a supportive learning environment.

Example: A math tutor working one-on-one with a student to improve their understanding of algebraic concepts.

Steps

1. **Assessment**: Identify the student's current level and areas of need.
2. **Set Goals**: Establish clear, achievable learning objectives.
3. **Instruction**: Provide tailored instruction and practice.
4. **Feedback**: Give immediate, specific feedback.
5. **Reassessment**: Evaluate progress and adjust instruction as needed.

Example: In language learning, a tutor might focus on specific grammar issues the student struggles with.

Criteria

- **Needs Assessment**: Understand the student's current knowledge and learning gaps.
- **Customized Plans**: Create individualized learning plans based on the student's needs.
- **Interactive Engagement**: Ensure active participation and engagement from the student.
- **Progress Monitoring**: Continuously assess progress and adapt teaching strategies accordingly.

Example: A reading tutor might use different texts and exercises depending on the student's reading level and interests.

Role of Teacher

- **Mentor**: Provides guidance, support, and encouragement.
- **Evaluator**: Continuously assesses student progress and adjusts instruction.
- **Resource Provider**: Supplies relevant materials and resources tailored to the student's needs.

Classroom Example: A teacher might spend part of the class period working individually with a student who needs extra help with writing skills.

Merits and Demerits

Merits:

- **Personalized Attention**: Individual needs are directly addressed.
- **Flexible Pace**: Instruction moves at the student's pace.
- **Enhanced Understanding**: Direct interaction clarifies misunderstandings quickly.

Example: A science tutor can help a student understand complex concepts through tailored explanations and hands-on activities.

Demerits:

- **Time-Consuming**: Requires significant time investment from the teacher.
- **Resource Intensive**: Can be costly in terms of materials and teacher time.
- **Limited Scope**: Typically focuses on specific subjects or skills rather than a broad curriculum.

Example: One-on-one tutoring might not be feasible for all students in a large classroom setting.

Classroom Scenarios:

Scenario 1: One-on-One Reading Session

- A teacher works one-on-one with a struggling reader, providing personalized instruction and feedback to improve their reading skills.

Scenario 2: Math Tutoring

- A student who needs extra help in math meets with the teacher for a weekly tutoring session to review concepts and practice problems.

Scenario 3: Writing Workshop

- In a writing class, the teacher provides individual feedback to each student on their essays, offering specific suggestions for improvement.

Scenario 4: Language Learning

- A language teacher meets with a student to practice conversation skills, focusing on pronunciation and fluency in a more personalized setting.

Scenario 5: Science Experiment Guidance

- During a lab session, the teacher provides one-on-one assistance to students conducting experiments, ensuring they understand the procedures and concepts.

19. Correlational / Integrative Method

Meaning: The correlational or integrative method involves making connections between different subjects or concepts to enhance understanding and provide a holistic view of the material.

Definitions by Experts:

1. **Drake and Burns (2004)**: "An integrative curriculum is a coherent and unified whole, organized around significant questions and ideas, rather than a collection of discrete subjects."

2. **Jacobs (1989)**: "Curriculum integration is a way of teaching and learning in which students broadly explore knowledge in various subjects related to certain aspects of their environment."

Purpose

Purpose: The purpose of the correlational method is to help students see the interconnections between different areas of knowledge, fostering a deeper understanding and promoting critical thinking.

Examples:

- A unit that integrates history, literature, and art to explore the Renaissance period.

- A project that combines science and math to investigate environmental issues.

Steps

1. **Identify Connections**:
   - o Determine the subjects or concepts that can be integrated.
   - o Identify the key questions or themes that connect them.

2. **Develop Curriculum**:
   - o Create a unified curriculum that incorporates the identified connections.
   - o Design activities and projects that explore the interconnected themes.

3. **Implementation**:
   - o Teach the integrated curriculum, emphasizing the connections between subjects.
   - o Use interdisciplinary activities to reinforce learning.

4. **Assessment**:
   - o Assess students' understanding of the integrated material.
   - o Use projects and presentations to evaluate their ability to make connections.

Criteria

1. **Relevance**:
   - o Ensure the integrated themes are meaningful and relevant to students.
   - o Connect the material to real-world issues and experiences.

2. **Coherence**:
   - o Create a cohesive curriculum that logically integrates different subjects.
   - o Ensure activities and assessments align with the integrated themes.

3. **Engagement**:
   - o Design engaging activities that highlight the connections between subjects.
   - o Encourage student exploration and inquiry.

4. **Critical Thinking**:
   - o Promote critical thinking by challenging students to see the bigger picture.
   - o Use questions and projects that require deep analysis and synthesis.

Role of Teacher

Examples:

- **Curriculum Designer**: Develops an integrated curriculum that connects different subjects.

- **Facilitator**: Guides students in exploring the connections between concepts.
- **Assessment Designer**: Creates assessments that evaluate students' understanding of the integrated material.

Merits and Demerits

Merits:

- **Holistic Understanding**: Helps students see the bigger picture and understand the interconnections between different areas of knowledge.
    - Example: A student understands how historical events influenced literature and art.
- **Engagement**: Makes learning more engaging by connecting material to real-world issues.
    - Example: A project that investigates the impact of pollution using science and math concepts.
- **Critical Thinking**: Promotes critical thinking and analysis.
    - Example: Students analyze the causes and effects of historical events from multiple perspectives.

Demerits:

- **Complexity**: Requires careful planning and coordination.

- o Example: A teacher must design a cohesive curriculum that effectively integrates different subjects.
- **Assessment Challenges**: Assessing integrated learning can be difficult.
  - o Example: Evaluating a student's ability to make connections between subjects requires more complex assessments.
- **Resource Intensive**: Demands significant time and resources to develop and implement.
  - o Example: A teacher spends considerable time developing interdisciplinary activities and projects.

Classroom Scenarios

1. **Interdisciplinary Unit**:
   - o A unit on the Renaissance that integrates history, literature, and art, with students exploring how these fields influenced each other during that period.
2. **Environmental Project**:
   - o Students work on a project that investigates environmental issues, using science to understand the problems and math to analyze data.
3. **STEM Integration**:
   - o A STEM project that combines science, technology, engineering, and math to design and build a prototype solution to a real-world problem.

4. **Social Studies and Literature**:

   o   Students read historical fiction novels and analyze how the historical context influences the story, integrating social studies and literature.

5. **Cross-Curricular Theme**:

   o   A school-wide theme, such as "sustainability," where students explore the theme in various subjects, including science, social studies, and art.

20. Constructivisit Method

Meaning: The constructivist method is based on the theory that learners construct their own understanding and knowledge of the world through experiences and reflection. It emphasizes active learning, where students build on their prior knowledge through exploration and inquiry.

Definitions by Experts:

1. **Piaget (1954)**: "Constructivism is the idea that knowledge is constructed by the learner based on mental activity."
2. **Vygotsky (1978)**: "Learning is a socially mediated activity, and knowledge is constructed through interaction with others."

Purpose

Purpose: The purpose of the constructivist method is to encourage students to take an active role in their learning, promoting critical thinking, problem-solving, and the ability to apply knowledge in real-world contexts.

Examples:

*   Students explore scientific concepts through hands-on experiments and draw conclusions based on their observations.

- A history class where students analyze primary sources and construct their own interpretations of historical events.

Steps

1. **Activate Prior Knowledge**:
   - Start by connecting new information to what students already know.
   - Use questions and activities to elicit prior knowledge.

2. **Engage in Exploration**:
   - Encourage students to explore concepts through hands-on activities and inquiry.
   - Provide opportunities for experimentation and discovery.

3. **Facilitate Reflection**:
   - Promote reflection on experiences and observations.
   - Use discussions and journals to help students articulate their understanding.

4. **Construct Knowledge**:
   - Guide students in constructing their own understanding and knowledge.
   - Encourage students to draw connections and synthesize information.

Criteria

1. **Active Engagement**:
    - Ensure students are actively engaged in the learning process.
    - Use interactive and hands-on activities to promote exploration.

2. **Reflection**:
    - Provide opportunities for students to reflect on their learning experiences.
    - Use discussions, journals, and other reflective activities.

3. **Collaboration**:
    - Encourage collaboration and interaction with peers.
    - Use group activities and discussions to facilitate knowledge construction.

4. **Application**:
    - Ensure students can apply their knowledge to real-world contexts.
    - Use projects and problem-solving activities that require application of concepts.

Role of Teacher

Examples:

- **Facilitator**: Guides students in exploring and constructing knowledge, rather than simply transmitting information.
- **Questioner**: Asks probing questions that encourage deeper thinking and exploration.
- **Support Provider**: Offers support and resources to aid students in their inquiry and reflection.

Merits and Demerits

Merits:

- **Promotes Deep Understanding**: Encourages students to construct their own understanding, leading to deeper learning.
  - Example: A student who experiments with different solutions to a problem gains a deeper understanding of the underlying concepts.
- **Enhances Critical Thinking**: Promotes critical thinking and problem-solving skills.
  - Example: Students analyzing historical sources develop critical thinking by evaluating evidence and forming their own interpretations.

- **Encourages Engagement**: Actively engages students in the learning process.
  - Example: A hands-on science experiment that captures students' interest and curiosity.

Demerits:

- **Time-Consuming**: Requires significant time for exploration and reflection.
  - Example: A project-based learning activity may take longer to complete compared to traditional instruction.
- **Requires Skilled Facilitation**: Demands skilled facilitation to guide students effectively.
  - Example: A teacher must be adept at asking probing questions and providing appropriate support.
- **Varied Outcomes**: Learning outcomes can vary widely among students.
  - Example: Students may construct different understandings based on their prior knowledge and experiences.

Classroom Scenarios

1. **Science Inquiry**:
   - Students conduct experiments to explore scientific concepts, drawing conclusions based on their observations and reflecting on their findings.

2. **History Analysis**:
   - Students analyze primary sources to construct their own interpretations of historical events, discussing their findings and reflecting on different perspectives.

3. **Mathematical Exploration**:
   - Students explore mathematical concepts through hands-on activities and problem-solving tasks, constructing their understanding through experimentation and reflection.

4. **Literature Discussion**:
   - Students read and discuss literature, sharing their interpretations and reflecting on different themes and perspectives.

5. **Project-Based Learning**:
   - Students work on a project that requires them to research a real-world problem, construct their understanding through inquiry and collaboration, and present their findings.

21. Socratice Questioning

Meaning: Socratic questioning is a method of teaching that involves asking a series of thought-provoking questions to stimulate critical thinking and draw out ideas and underlying presumptions. It is based on the teaching method used by Socrates, who engaged his students in dialogue to help them develop their understanding.

Definitions by Experts:

1. **Paul and Elder (2006)**: "Socratic questioning is disciplined questioning that can be used to pursue thought in many directions and for many purposes, including to explore complex ideas, to get to the truth of things, to open up issues and problems, to uncover assumptions, to analyze concepts, and to distinguish what we know from what we do not know."

2. **Brookfield (2012)**: "Socratic questioning is a systematic approach to understanding that involves asking deep, probing questions to encourage reflective and critical thinking."

Purpose

Purpose: The purpose of Socratic questioning is to develop critical thinking skills, encourage deep reflection, and help students uncover their assumptions and beliefs. It aims to foster a deeper understanding and stimulate intellectual curiosity.

Examples:

- A philosophy class where the teacher asks students to examine their beliefs about justice through a series of probing questions.
- A literature class where students analyze a text by answering questions that explore the author's intent and the characters' motivations.

Steps

1. **Pose an Initial Question**:
   - Begin with a broad, open-ended question to introduce the topic.
   - Example: "What is justice?"

2. **Ask Probing Questions**:
   - Follow up with deeper, more specific questions that challenge assumptions and encourage critical thinking.
   - Example: "Why do you think justice is important in society?"

3. **Encourage Reflection**:
   - Encourage students to reflect on their answers and consider different perspectives.

- o Example: "Can you think of a situation where what is just might differ from what is legal?"

4. **Facilitate Dialogue**:
   - o Promote dialogue among students, encouraging them to ask questions and respond to each other.
   - o Example: "How does your view of justice compare to your classmates' views?"

5. **Summarize and Reflect**:
   - o Summarize the discussion and encourage further reflection.
   - o Example: "Based on our discussion, how has your understanding of justice evolved?"

Criteria

1. **Open-Ended Questions**:
   - o Use questions that require more than a yes or no answer, encouraging deep thinking.
   - o Ensure questions stimulate exploration and inquiry.

2. **Probing and Clarifying**:
   - o Ask questions that probe deeper into students' responses, seeking clarification and elaboration.
   - o Challenge assumptions and encourage critical analysis.

3. **Encouraging Reflection**:
   - o Promote reflection on responses and encourage consideration of different perspectives.
   - o Use questions that require students to think deeply and reflect on their beliefs.

4. **Facilitating Dialogue**:
   - o Encourage dialogue among students, promoting a collaborative learning environment.
   - o Use questions that stimulate discussion and exchange of ideas.

Role of Teacher

Examples:

- **Facilitator**: Guides the discussion through carefully crafted questions, encouraging deep thinking and reflection.
- **Questioner**: Asks probing questions that challenge students' assumptions and stimulate critical thinking.
- **Summarizer**: Summarizes the discussion, highlighting key points and encouraging further reflection.

Merits and Demerits

Merits:

- **Promotes Critical Thinking**: Encourages students to think deeply and critically about complex issues.

- o Example: Students develop a more nuanced understanding of ethical dilemmas through Socratic questioning.

- **Encourages Active Learning**: Engages students in the learning process through dialogue and inquiry.
  - o Example: A literature class where students analyze a text through Socratic questioning becomes more interactive and engaging.

- **Develops Communication Skills**: Enhances students' ability to articulate their thoughts and engage in meaningful dialogue.
  - o Example: Students improve their ability to express their ideas and respond to others' viewpoints.

Demerits:

- **Time-Consuming**: Requires significant time for in-depth questioning and discussion.
  - o Example: A single Socratic questioning session may take up an entire class period.

- **May Cause Discomfort**: Students may feel uncomfortable or challenged by probing questions.
  - o Example: A student may feel exposed or defensive when asked to justify their beliefs.

- **Varied Participation**: Not all students may participate equally, leading to uneven engagement.

- o Example: More vocal students may dominate the discussion, while others may remain silent.

Classroom Scenarios

1. **Philosophy Discussion**:
   - o A teacher uses Socratic questioning to explore philosophical concepts, asking students to examine their beliefs about ethics and morality.

2. **Literature Analysis**:
   - o Students analyze a literary text through Socratic questioning, exploring themes, characters, and the author's intent.

3. **Science Inquiry**:
   - o A teacher uses Socratic questioning to explore scientific concepts, asking students to examine their understanding of a scientific theory and its implications.

4. **History Debate**:
   - o Students engage in a Socratic questioning session to analyze historical events, considering different perspectives and interpretations.

5. **Math Problem-Solving**:
   - o A teacher uses Socratic questioning to guide students through a complex math problem, encouraging them to think critically about their approach and solutions.

22. Theme Based Learning

Meaning: Theme-based learning is an instructional approach that integrates various subjects and learning activities around a central theme. This method allows students to explore and connect different areas of knowledge through a common topic, fostering deeper understanding and engagement.

Definitions by Experts:

1. **Fogarty (1991)**: "Theme-based learning is an instructional strategy that organizes the curriculum around themes that are meaningful and relevant to students, integrating different subject areas and promoting holistic learning."
2. **Beane (1997)**: "Theme-based learning involves designing the curriculum around themes that cut across subject lines and encourage students to make connections between different areas of knowledge."

Purpose

Purpose: The purpose of theme-based learning is to create a more engaging and cohesive learning experience by integrating multiple subjects around a central theme. This approach aims to promote deeper understanding, critical thinking, and the ability to apply knowledge in various contexts.

Examples:

- A theme on "Environmental Conservation" that integrates science (ecosystems, pollution), social studies (environmental policies, community actions), and language arts (writing persuasive essays, reading related literature).
- A theme on "Space Exploration" that combines science (astronomy, physics), math (calculations, measurements), and art (creating space-themed projects).

Steps

1. **Select a Central Theme**:
   - Choose a theme that is relevant, interesting, and broad enough to integrate multiple subjects.
   - Example: "Sustainability and Green Living."
2. **Identify Key Concepts and Objectives**:
   - Determine the key concepts and learning objectives related to the theme.
   - Example: "Understand the principles of sustainability, the impact of human activities on the environment, and ways to reduce our ecological footprint."
3. **Plan Integrated Activities**:
   - Design activities and projects that integrate various subjects around the theme.

- o Example: "Science experiments on renewable energy, social studies projects on sustainable communities, and art projects using recycled materials."

4. **Implement and Facilitate**:

- o Facilitate the activities, guiding students as they explore the theme and make connections between subjects.
- o Example: "Guide students through a project on creating a sustainable school garden, integrating science, math, and social studies."

5. **Assess and Reflect**:

- o Assess students' understanding and skills, and encourage reflection on their learning experiences.
- o Example: "Evaluate students' projects and presentations, and conduct a reflection session on what they learned about sustainability."

Criteria

1. **Relevance**:

- o Ensure the theme is relevant to students' interests and experiences.
- o Example: "Choose a theme like 'Healthy Living' that resonates with students' daily lives."

2. **Integration**:
   - Integrate multiple subjects and learning activities around the theme.
   - Example: "Combine science (nutrition), physical education (exercise), and language arts (writing about healthy habits)."

3. **Engagement**:
   - Design activities that actively engage students and encourage participation.
   - Example: "Plan hands-on activities like cooking healthy meals or conducting fitness challenges."

4. **Reflection and Assessment**:
   - Include opportunities for reflection and assessment to reinforce learning.
   - Example: "Have students keep a journal of their healthy living activities and reflect on their progress."

Role of Teacher

Examples:

- **Facilitator**: Guides students through the theme-based activities, helping them make connections between different subjects.
- **Designer**: Plans and organizes the integrated curriculum around the central theme.

- **Evaluator**: Assesses students' understanding and skills through various forms of assessment and reflection.

Merits and Demerits

Merits:

- **Promotes Holistic Learning**: Integrates multiple subjects, promoting a comprehensive understanding of the theme.
  - Example: Students learn about sustainability through science, social studies, and art, gaining a well-rounded perspective.
- **Increases Engagement**: Engages students by connecting learning to their interests and real-world issues.
  - Example: A theme on "Space Exploration" captures students' imagination and enthusiasm.
- **Encourages Critical Thinking**: Promotes critical thinking and the ability to make connections between different areas of knowledge.
  - Example: Students analyze the impact of human activities on the environment and propose solutions.

Demerits:

- **Planning Intensive**: Requires significant planning and coordination to integrate multiple subjects effectively.

- o Example: Teachers need to collaborate to design a cohesive and comprehensive theme-based curriculum.
- **Varied Pacing**: Students may progress at different rates, making it challenging to ensure all students achieve the learning objectives.
  - o Example: Some students may need more time to grasp complex concepts, while others may move ahead quickly.
- **Assessment Challenges**: Assessing integrated learning outcomes can be complex and time-consuming.
  - o Example: Teachers need to develop assessment tools that capture the depth and breadth of students' understanding.

Classroom Scenarios

1. **Environmental Conservation**:
   - o Students explore the theme of environmental conservation through science experiments on pollution, social studies projects on environmental policies, and language arts activities writing persuasive essays on conservation efforts.
2. **Space Exploration**:
   - o The theme of space exploration is integrated into the curriculum, with science lessons on astronomy, math

activities calculating space travel distances, and art projects creating space-themed artworks.

3. **Healthy Living**:
   - o Students learn about healthy living through integrated activities such as science lessons on nutrition, physical education fitness challenges, and language arts writing about healthy habits.

4. **Cultural Heritage**:
   - o A theme on cultural heritage includes social studies research on different cultures, art projects creating cultural artifacts, and language arts activities writing stories or reports about cultural traditions.

5. **Community Service**:
   - o Students engage in a theme-based learning project on community service, with social studies lessons on civic responsibility, language arts activities writing proposals for community projects, and math activities planning and budgeting for community events.

Conclusion

Theme-based learning is an effective instructional approach that fosters holistic learning, engagement, and critical thinking. By integrating multiple subjects around a central theme, teachers can create a cohesive and meaningful learning experience that connects classroom learning to real-world issues and students' interests.

23. Project Method

Meaning: The project method is a teaching approach where students engage in in-depth investigation and problem-solving on a particular topic or question. It emphasizes active learning, collaboration, and the application of knowledge to real-world situations.

Definitions by Experts:

1. **Kilpatrick (1918)**: "The project method is a purposeful activity, carried out with the intention of solving a problem or answering a question, and results in a tangible product or outcome."
2. **Dewey (1938)**: "The project method involves learning by doing, where students actively engage in projects that are meaningful and relevant to their interests and experiences."

Purpose

Purpose: The purpose of the project method is to promote deep understanding, critical thinking, and problem-solving skills. It encourages students to take ownership of their learning, collaborate with peers, and apply their knowledge in practical contexts.

Examples:

- A science project where students investigate the effects of pollution on local ecosystems.

- A history project where students research and create a presentation on a significant historical event.

Steps

1. **Identify the Topic**:
   - Choose a topic or question that is meaningful and relevant to students.
   - Example: "Investigate the impact of plastic pollution on marine life."

2. **Plan the Project**:
   - Develop a plan that outlines the project's objectives, activities, and timeline.
   - Example: "Create a project plan that includes research, data collection, and presentation."

3. **Conduct Research and Investigation**:
   - Engage in research, data collection, and experimentation related to the project topic.
   - Example: "Collect data on plastic waste in local water bodies and analyze its effects on marine life."

4. **Create the Product**:
   - Develop a tangible product or outcome that demonstrates students' learning and findings.
   - Example: "Create a report and presentation on the impact of plastic pollution, including recommendations for reducing waste."

5. **Present and Reflect**:
   - o Present the project findings to peers, teachers, or the community, and reflect on the learning process.
   - o Example: "Present the project to the class and discuss the implications of the findings and potential solutions."

Criteria

1. **Relevance and Interest**:
   - o Ensure the project topic is relevant to students' interests and experiences.
   - o Example: "Choose a project topic that aligns with students' passions and curiosities."

2. **Collaboration**:
   - o Promote collaboration and teamwork throughout the project.
   - o Example: "Encourage students to work in groups and share responsibilities."

3. **Depth of Investigation**:
   - o Encourage thorough research and investigation on the project topic.
   - o Example: "Require students to use multiple sources and methods for data collection."

4. **Application of Knowledge**:

   - o Ensure students apply their knowledge and skills to real-world situations.
   - o Example: "Design projects that require students to solve real-world problems or answer complex questions."

Role of Teacher

Examples:

- **Facilitator**: Guides students through the project process, providing support and resources as needed.
- **Coach**: Offers feedback and advice to help students stay on track and achieve their project goals.
- **Evaluator**: Assesses students' progress and final products, providing constructive feedback.

Merits and Demerits

Merits:

- **Promotes Deep Learning**: Encourages in-depth investigation and understanding of complex topics.
  - o Example: Students gain a deep understanding of environmental issues through a pollution project.

- **Develops Critical Skills**: Enhances critical thinking, problem-solving, and collaboration skills.
  - Example: Students develop teamwork and research skills through group projects.
- **Engages and Motivates**: Engages students by allowing them to explore topics of interest and relevance.
  - Example: A project on renewable energy captures students' interest and motivates them to learn.

Demerits:

- **Time-Consuming**: Requires significant time for planning, research, and execution.
  - Example: A comprehensive project may take several weeks to complete.
- **Resource Intensive**: Demands access to resources, materials, and support.
  - Example: Students may need access to research materials, technology, and guidance.
- **Varied Outcomes**: Learning outcomes can vary widely among students.
  - Example: Different groups may produce varying levels of quality and depth in their projects.

Classroom Scenarios

1. **Science Project**:
   - o Students investigate the effects of pollution on local ecosystems, collecting data and presenting their findings.

2. **History Project**:
   - o Students research a significant historical event and create a multimedia presentation on their findings.

3. **Math Project**:
   - o Students explore real-world applications of mathematical concepts, such as calculating the cost of building a structure or analyzing statistical data.

4. **Art Project**:
   - o Students create a collaborative art project that explores a particular theme or concept, such as cultural diversity or environmental conservation.

5. **Community Service Project**:
   - o Students design and implement a community service project, such as organizing a recycling program or conducting a neighborhood clean-up.

24. Programmed Instruction

Meaning: Programmed instruction is a systematic method of teaching that uses carefully designed instructional materials to present information in small, sequential steps, allowing students to progress at their own pace and receive immediate feedback.

Definitions by Experts:

1. **Skinner (1958)**: "Programmed instruction is a method of presenting instructional content in a carefully structured and sequenced manner, allowing for self-paced learning and immediate reinforcement."
2. **Lumsdaine (1964)**: "Programmed instruction involves the use of teaching machines or materials that present information in small steps, requiring active student responses and providing immediate feedback."

Purpose

Purpose: The purpose of programmed instruction is to facilitate individualized learning, allowing students to progress at their own pace, receive immediate feedback, and achieve mastery of the material through systematic and structured instruction.

Examples:

- A language learning program that presents vocabulary and grammar in small, incremental steps, with practice exercises and immediate feedback.
- A math tutorial program that guides students through problem-solving techniques, providing hints and feedback at each step.

Steps

1. **Design Instructional Material**:
   - Develop instructional content that is broken down into small, manageable steps.
   - Example: "Create a language learning program with sequential lessons on vocabulary and grammar."

2. **Present Information**:
   - Present information in a clear, structured, and sequential manner.
   - Example: "Introduce new vocabulary words one at a time, with definitions and examples."

3. **Require Active Response**:
   - Design activities that require students to actively engage with the material and respond to questions or exercises.
   - Example: "Include practice exercises where students must use new vocabulary in sentences."

4. **Provide Immediate Feedback**:

   o Offer immediate feedback on students' responses, reinforcing correct answers and providing guidance on incorrect ones.

   o Example: "Provide instant feedback on practice exercises, highlighting correct usage and explaining mistakes."

5. **Allow Self-Paced Progression**:

   o Enable students to progress through the material at their own pace, ensuring they achieve mastery before moving on.

   o Example: "Allow students to move to the next lesson only after successfully completing the current one."

Criteria

1. **Sequential Presentation**:

   o Ensure the material is presented in a logical and sequential order.

   o Example: "Introduce basic concepts before moving on to more complex topics."

2. **Active Engagement**:

   o Design activities that require active student engagement and response.

   o Example: "Include interactive exercises that require students to apply what they've learned."

3. **Immediate Feedback**:

- o Provide immediate feedback to reinforce learning and correct misunderstandings.
- o Example: "Use automated feedback systems to provide instant responses to student answers."

4. **Self-Paced Learning**:

- o Allow students to progress through the material at their own pace, ensuring mastery of each step.
- o Example: "Design the program to allow students to review and repeat lessons as needed."

Role of Teacher

Examples:

- **Designer**: Develops and organizes the instructional material in a systematic and structured manner.
- **Facilitator**: Supports students as they work through the material, providing guidance and assistance as needed.
- **Evaluator**: Assesses students' progress and provides additional resources or support as necessary.

Merits and Demerits

Merits:

- **Individualized Learning**: Allows students to learn at their own pace and according to their individual needs.

- o Example: A student struggling with a particular concept can spend more time on it without feeling rushed.
- **Immediate Feedback**: Provides immediate reinforcement and correction, enhancing learning and retention.
  - o Example: Students receive instant feedback on their answers, helping them understand their mistakes and learn from them.
- **Consistency**: Ensures consistent delivery of instructional content.
  - o Example: All students receive the same structured and sequenced material, ensuring uniformity in learning.

Demerits:

- **Limited Interaction**: May reduce opportunities for teacher-student and student-student interaction.
  - o Example: A programmed instruction program may not provide opportunities for group discussions or collaborative learning.
- **Potential for Boredom**: The structured and sequential nature may become monotonous for some students.
  - o Example: Students may lose interest if the material is too repetitive or lacks engagement.
- **Requires Self-Motivation**: Students need to be self-motivated to progress through the material independently.

o Example: Students who lack self-discipline may struggle to keep up with the program.

Classroom Scenarios

1. **Language Learning Program**:
   o Students use a language learning program that presents vocabulary and grammar lessons in small, sequential steps, with practice exercises and immediate feedback.

2. **Math Tutorial Program**:
   o Students work through a math tutorial program that guides them through problem-solving techniques, providing hints and feedback at each step.

3. **Science Concept Review**:
   o Students use a programmed instruction program to review key science concepts, with interactive exercises and immediate feedback.

4. **History Fact Mastery**:
   o Students engage with a history program that presents key events and dates in a structured, sequential manner, with quizzes and feedback.

5. **Typing Skills Practice**:
   o Students use a typing program that teaches keyboarding skills through structured lessons and immediate feedback on their typing speed and accuracy.

25. Heuristic Method

Meaning: The heuristic method is a teaching approach that encourages students to discover and learn through exploration, experimentation, and problem-solving. It emphasizes the development of independent thinking, creativity, and the ability to apply knowledge in new situations.

Definitions by Experts:

1. **Dewey (1933)**: "Heuristic methods involve learning through discovery and self-directed inquiry, encouraging students to explore, experiment, and draw conclusions based on their observations."

2. **Bruner (1961)**: "The heuristic method is a process of problem-solving that allows students to learn by finding solutions through exploration and experimentation."

Purpose

Purpose: The purpose of the heuristic method is to promote active learning, critical thinking, and problem-solving skills. It encourages students to take an active role in their learning, develop their own understanding, and apply their knowledge to new and unfamiliar situations.

Examples:

- A science experiment where students design their own investigations to explore a scientific concept.
- A math problem-solving activity where students develop their own strategies to solve complex problems.

Steps

1. **Identify the Problem or Question**:
   - o Present a problem or question that requires exploration and investigation.
   - o Example: "Investigate the effects of different variables on plant growth."

2. **Encourage Exploration and Inquiry**:
   - o Encourage students to explore, ask questions, and gather information related to the problem.
   - o Example: "Students brainstorm different factors that might affect plant growth and design experiments to test their hypotheses."

3. **Facilitate Experimentation**:
   - o Provide opportunities for students to experiment, test their ideas, and gather data.
   - o Example: "Students conduct experiments to test the effects of light, water, and soil on plant growth."

4. **Analyze and Reflect**:

- o Guide students in analyzing their data, drawing conclusions, and reflecting on their findings.
- o Example: "Students analyze their experimental results, draw conclusions about the effects of different variables, and reflect on the process."

5. **Apply Knowledge**:
   - o Encourage students to apply their knowledge and findings to new situations or problems.
   - o Example: "Students use their understanding of plant growth to design a plan for a school garden."

Criteria

1. **Student-Centered**:
   - o Ensure the approach is student-centered, allowing for exploration and self-directed learning.
   - o Example: "Students take the lead in designing and conducting experiments."

2. **Active Engagement**:
   - o Promote active engagement and hands-on learning.
   - o Example: "Students actively participate in experiments and data collection."

3. **Critical Thinking**:
   - o Encourage critical thinking and problem-solving.
   - o Example: "Students analyze data and draw conclusions based on evidence."

4. **Application of Knowledge**:
   - o Ensure students can apply their knowledge to new and unfamiliar situations.
   - o Example: "Students use their findings to solve real-world problems."

Role of Teacher

Examples:

- **Facilitator**: Guides and supports students in their exploration and experimentation, providing resources and guidance as needed.
- **Mentor**: Offers advice and feedback, helping students develop their problem-solving skills and understanding.
- **Evaluator**: Assesses students' progress and understanding, providing constructive feedback and opportunities for reflection.

Merits:

- **Promotes Independent Thinking**: Encourages students to think independently and develop their own understanding.
  - o Example: Students design their own experiments and draw their own conclusions.

- **Enhances Problem-Solving Skills**: Develops students' ability to solve complex problems through exploration and experimentation.
  - o Example: Students develop strategies for solving math problems through trial and error.
- **Encourages Creativity**: Fosters creativity and innovation in learning.
  - o Example: Students design unique experiments and explore new ideas.

Demerits:

- **Time-Consuming**: Requires significant time for exploration, experimentation, and reflection.
  - o Example: A single science experiment may take several class periods to complete.
- **Requires Resources**: Needs access to appropriate resources and materials for experimentation.
  - o Example: Students may need access to lab equipment, materials, and data collection tools.
- **Varied Outcomes**: Learning outcomes can vary widely among students.
  - o Example: Different students may draw different conclusions from their experiments.

Classroom Scenarios

1. **Science Experiment**:
   - o Students design and conduct their own experiments to investigate the effects of different variables on plant growth.

2. **Math Problem-Solving**:
   - o Students develop their own strategies for solving complex math problems, experimenting with different approaches and solutions.

3. **History Investigation**:
   - o Students explore a historical event or period, gathering information, analyzing evidence, and drawing conclusions based on their research.

4. **Art Exploration**:
   - o Students experiment with different art techniques and materials, creating original works of art based on their discoveries.

5. **Engineering Design Challenge**:
   - o Students design and build a prototype to solve a real-world engineering problem, testing their ideas and refining their designs based on their findings.

Epilogue

As we conclude this comprehensive exploration of various teaching methods, it becomes evident that the landscape of education is rich and diverse, continually evolving to meet the needs of learners in an ever-changing world. Each method discussed in this book—from traditional lectures to innovative experiential learning, from problem-based approaches to digital and online techniques—offers unique advantages and addresses different aspects of the learning process.

The journey through these teaching methods reveals a common thread: the profound commitment to fostering an environment where students can thrive. Whether through the structured guidance of scaffolding, the collaborative spirit of project-based learning, or the immersive experiences of fieldwork, each method emphasizes the importance of engaging students, nurturing their curiosity, and developing their critical thinking skills.

Educators play a pivotal role in this endeavor. Their ability to adapt, innovate, and personalize instruction is crucial in unlocking the potential of each student. The examples and scenarios provided throughout this book illustrate how teachers can effectively implement these methods, tailoring their approaches to the unique needs of their students and the specific goals of their courses.

The merits and demerits of each method underscore that there is no one-size-fits-all approach to teaching. Instead, effective education requires a blend of strategies, thoughtfully selected and skillfully applied. By understanding the strengths and limitations of each method, educators can create a balanced and dynamic classroom environment that supports diverse learning styles and promotes comprehensive understanding.

As we move forward, the continued evolution of teaching methods will undoubtedly be shaped by technological advancements, emerging research, and the changing needs of society. Educators must remain lifelong learners themselves, staying abreast of new developments and continually refining their practices to provide the best possible education for their students.

In closing, this book serves as a resource and inspiration for educators, encouraging them to explore, experiment, and embrace a variety of teaching methods. By doing so, they can cultivate a love of learning in their students, prepare them for the challenges of the future, and contribute to the development of thoughtful, informed, and capable individuals.

May this exploration of teaching methods empower educators to make meaningful impacts in their classrooms and beyond, fostering a brighter future for all learners.

References

1. **Bruner, J. S. (1978).** The Process of Education. Harvard University Press.

2. **Dewey, J. (1938).** Experience and Education. Collier Books.

3. **Fosnot, C. T. (1996).** Constructivism: Theory, Perspectives, and Practice. Teachers College Press.

4. **Kolb, D. A. (1984).** Experiential Learning: Experience as the Source of Learning and Development. Prentice-Hall.

5. **Prince, M. (2004).** Does Active Learning Work? A Review of the Research. Journal of Engineering Education, 93(3), 223-231.

6. **Savery, J. R. & Duffy, T. M. (1995).** Problem Based Learning: An Instructional Model and its Constructivist Framework. Educational Technology, 35(5), 31-38.

7. **Schunk, D. H. (2012).** Learning Theories: An Educational Perspective. Pearson.

8. **Slavin, R. E. (1996).** Educational Psychology: Theory and Practice. Allyn & Bacon.

9. **Vygotsky, L. S. (1978).** Mind in Society: The Development of Higher Psychological Processes. Harvard University Press.

10. **Wiggins, G. & McTighe, J. (2005).** Understanding by Design. ASCD.

11. **Wood, D., Bruner, J. S., & Ross, G. (1976).** The Role of Tutoring in Problem Solving. Journal of Child Psychology and Psychiatry, 17(2), 89-100.

12. **Zull, J. E. (2002).** The Art of Changing the Brain: Enriching the Practice of Teaching by Exploring the Biology of Learning. Stylus Publishing.

Online Resources

1. **Edutopia**. (n.d.). Retrieved from https://www.edutopia.org

2. **Harvard Graduate School of Education**. (n.d.). Retrieved from https://www.gse.harvard.edu

3. **Khan Academy**. (n.d.). Retrieved from https://www.khanacademy.org

4. **National Education Association**. (n.d.). Retrieved from https://www.nea.org

5. **TeachThought**. (n.d.). Retrieved from https://www.teachthought.com